Then Joy Breaks Through

D0809574

George Benson, M.D.

Thanks to my wife,
Virginia Perkins Benson,
for her professional editorial skills
and her encouragement.

Contents

Chapter 8

Introduction

The subject of this book is the original and continuing power of the Christian faith to enable men and women to grow away from guilt toward affirmation; away from fragmentation toward wholeness; and away from despair toward joy. The Christian faith is much more than personal growth, but in a world that is exploding with new information, new problems and new possibilities, faith is tenable only if it can produce renewed and maturing believers. This is why sincere Christians who have accepted their faith as an unexamined gift from preceding generations are increasingly anxious; the faith they have inherited often strives toward placid stability rather than personal change and development in response to new facts and insights.

In any age, faith must be validated by the personal experiences of the believer and not by inherited precepts. However, experience alone is not enough. Faith that moves and develops us rather than just maintains us is validated only by experiences and conclusions that are constantly questioned. When unquestioned, new ideas and insights which arise from experience only confirm the comforting convictions of worried people who seek in their faith the security of fixation rather than change, the certainty of immobility rather than growth. Such people must shy away from new concepts and changing feelings. Under the guise of "keeping the faith" they must deny the fresh and growing parts of their own personality.

The unshakable, unchanging faith of yesterday's great leaders taught us to rely on the experience of others rather than examine ourselves. But in today's heterogeneous, exposed, and painfully informed society, the security and certainty of a solidified personal faith can only be sustained by Christians who deliberately turn away from the stimulating beliefs and experiences of others. Today's unchanging faith is simply unchallenged faith. And so, paradoxically, today's Christians who seek the peace and serenity of yesterday's faith are anxiously conflicted. In the name of faith they disregard the ideas and experiences of others only to find themselves in a position of utter isolation.

Today's Christians who seek yesterday's objectives are torn not only because they must live fragmented within themselves but because they must live separated from their brothers and sisters. They live in fear of stimulation and confrontation from outside and from within themselves. Such Christians are increasingly anxious because there is no way for them to remain naive and yet be honest with themselves; no way to be unchanging and yet be responsibly related to Christ. It is also true that believers must find a creative place in their faith for today's knowledge. Otherwise, they risk demeaning themselves by dulling the reflective and intellectual powers they must demonstrate if they are to be taken seriously by the moving world.

If today's Christian faith is to be more than a comforting fiction, then today's Christians must rediscover their ancient forebearers' capacity to find growth and strength in doubt and anxiety, new development in disappointment, and greater freedom in new facts. If today's church and Christians are to be more than a pathetic paradox, then today's faith must have a better foundation than bliss predicated on isolation. It must be a basis for personal growth, a basis for new life that is enriched by new facts and deepened by new awareness.

New life is a core message of the Christian gospel, but modern Christians seem more fearful of it and less dynamic in their approach to the subject than their unchurched sisters and brothers. Detractors and pessimists offer simplistic notions which explain, to their own satisfaction, the church's adynamic approach to the subject of personal growth. The church's present existence as well as its two-thousand-year history can be made to support any catalog of faults and errors one chooses to compile. But these lists of grievances obviously do not help the church. Neither are efforts of many dedicated and informed Christians simply to bypass the problem of personal growth and attempt instead to work with one of the church's crucial social objectives, as helpful as they mean to be.

For example, it is often claimed by a sincere avant-garde of such people that the church is declining because of its failure to offer meaningful leadership to the current social reform movement. They conclude that the church is not only irrelevant to the poor and those who suffer injustice but to all whose lives are depreciated by "the system." But the church is not irrelevant to the contemporary social, political and economic world because it has failed to do its social work. The church has not done its social work because it has become irrelevant to the needs of men and women who want their lives to be "in process." These are the people who are willing and able to speak to issues with telling effectiveness because they find in their faith freedom from ghettos of mind that restrict others.

Other tangential observers of the present scene account for the church's troubled condition in terms of the attitudes of its clergy toward the vicissitudes of their work. For example, they point out that quite contrary to their ancient predecessors, many modern priests and ministers seem painfully burdened by the idea that they must be universally loved and accepted by their parishioners. To these clergy, criticism is a clear indication that their surpassing good will is unappreciated, and opposition to their efforts is evidence that they are unliked. But this is not only a problem of clergy; it is an example of the immaturity which afflicts all Christendom.

The capacity of the Christian faith to ferment continuing personal change is too centrally important to be explained away. It is too vitally important to every endeavor of the church to be bypassed by compassionate people who are too preoccupied with the world's pain to understand the fundamental causes of that pain. In their ardent efforts these people do not see that today's "good works" will soon be seen by the recipients as belittling and infuriating charity unless they are carried out by people whose personal lives are constantly moving toward more honest concern and more knowledgeable love.

So this is a book about the growth factor in the Christian faith and the human difficulties Christians have in responding to it. This is not a simplistic translation of theological concepts into psychological terms. Such works glibly assume that psychological explanations are intrinsically more meaningful. But I reject the dangerous notion that psychodynamic explanations of human thinking necessarily reveal the essence of that thinking.

Psychological jargon has reached such enormous popularity that many people automatically conclude that because they interpret something in psychological terms, they understand it in its most essential aspects. It is like saying that a piece of newspaper blowing across a darkened street is indeed a mad dog, because the anxieties and conflicts of the observer have led him to respond as if he were being chased. The way one perceives a piece of paper will determine one's response to it, but one's perception does not change the characteristics of the paper. Hence, there is a vast difference between describing various human responses to religious faith and assuming that faith is nothing more than the human responses it evokes. To study human responses and perceptions, one must only recognize the value of understanding human beings. But to describe religious faith simply in terms of human psychology, one must accept the notion that the reality toward which religious faith strives is nothing more than a system of highly variable and unreliable human responses.

When the object of human responses cannot be analyzed in familiar terms, modern people are as uncomfortable in their mystification as were their ancestors. In haste they set aside the methods of science and fill the gaps in their understanding with fantasy.

As sane people once declared the town eccentric to be a witch because young girls reacted to her as girls were known to react to witches, learned men and women of our time declare God dead because people respond as if he did not exist. We cannot examine God as we can a piece of newspaper, so we assume that unlike anything else in the universe, descriptions of the deity based solely on psychological responses are reliable.

It is true that the infinite realities which faith tries to comprehend are neither created nor destroyed by our response to them; but without personal growth, the practitioners of unexplored faith quickly become shallow people. Shallow people do not change or nullify eternal verities, but neither can they respond to them. To the immature, the most challenging truths comprehensible by the human mind appear to be nothing more than a winsome collection of helpful rules and comforting stories that change nothing and no one. But growing men and women, because they are constantly renewed, see their faith as a compelling and creative force essential to their lives. Personal growth is the only frame of reference from which the Christian faith makes sense in our modern world.

Irrespective of the enormous emphasis Christian people have always laid on the supernatural aspects of their faith, the state of dynamic change and growth which characterized the lives of the apostles depended entirely on natural, understandable processes. To make this point, I have compared the change brought about by means of a classical psychoanalysis in the life of a despairing, dropped-out, teenage girl with the change brought about in the life of the apostle Peter in response to his relationship with Christ.[1] In the course of demonstrating the natural phenomena that are common denominators in the change which these apparently dissimilar people experienced, the book examines the success or failure of modern Christians to respond to the awesome natural forces which still undergird the Christian experience of new life.

---

[1] A word about confidentiality is in order, since the public reporting of private facts has grown to such ominous proportions in recent times. Meticulous care has been taken to preserve the privacy of persons who have worked with me in a confidential relationship. None of the episodes related in the book could possibly reveal the identity of any individual. By and large, the case material is related in the same way that a competent musician can play folk tunes (which are common property) in the style of Mozart. The music he plays is not original, but he could not play it if he did not know the heart and mind of Mozart utterly. The events of the life of Becky are like common tunes which I shall relate in the style of a nineteen-year-old girl from a middle class, religious family, a style with which long experience has thoroughly acquainted me.

Chapter 1

Becky: A Paradox in Action

Becky was nineteen. Obviously, she had once been pretty; but when she presented herself in my office, her blonde hair was matted with dirt and her teeth were yellow from lack of care. She was barefoot and dressed in ragged blue jeans and a stained work shirt.

At times she was excited to the point of thinking more rapidly than she could talk; at times she was nonchalant and arrogant; at times she was frightened and beseeching. Irrespective of her moods, however, everything she said was, to one degree or another, a test of my reliability. She would alternate between taking nothing for granted and then losing the details of her thoughts in a blur of generalizations. Feelings of closeness were expressed and then dissipated with broad, impersonal statements. Just as it appeared that I was getting to know Becky, she would become picky and argumentative. As we worked on her problems, her appearance became more bedraggled. By all ordinary standards, Becky was better off before treatment.

Initially, she complained of chronic depression. Depression meant, "I can't get my head together," and "Everything is a drag." Drugs—LSD, marijuana, and speed—offered some relief from pain, but they were also frightening. She could never quite forget the terror of having taken an overdose of heroin while on a trip to Mexico.

The circumstances of that experience seemed almost calculated to be humiliating. To buy the drug she cleaned toilets in a rooming house for a month. As she told me how she remembered "just dying to get home," it became apparent that she was, for the first time in months, sincere. The sincerity expressed in that memory was also apparent to Becky. It unnerved her, and so the following sessions were filled with disdain, doubts about the treatment, and scornful accusations of my coldness. As if to remind us both that she was hopeless, she recalled having sold drugs to high school kids. And as if that were not bad enough, she confessed to having sold "fake" drugs to the kids who were naive enough to "get high on colored water."

Becky's deeply religious family was falling apart under the strain of her delinquency. Obviously, she was as unable to understand the disintegrating process she appeared to have introduced into the family as were her mother and father. But she did know one thing that they did not know. Becky knew that she felt more pain over what had happened than anyone else. Her parents could not know this because every possible approach to their daughter's true feelings was sealed off and covered over with a variety of falsified feelings. Perhaps the most isolating of her affected emotions was truculence. Her truculence pushed people who tried to be patient with her to unnatural limits of endurance, and then they were discounted as insincere. People who responded with anger were not taken seriously either, because they appeared to be "uncaring." Eventually everyone who tried to help fell into one or another category.

Perhaps the only reason she continued treatment was

the advantage I had in not being identified in the patient's mind with the chronic "virtue and goodness" characteristic of her family. This was important to me also because, freed of this, I was able to realize that the problem could not be understood simply in terms of Becky's failure to develop as her parents expected. Her problems were not a matter of her failing to live up to family standards; they were a matter of her being driven to destroy her chances to live up to her own standards. Of course, Becky refused to see it that way. Whenever I interpreted her thoughts and behavior in terms of her compulsive urge to destroy herself, she accused me of trying to con her into "making something of myself." I pointed out that such an interpretation of my efforts was in itself an example of her need to construe things in such a way as to ruin her hopes of being helped; that is, if I were a con artist, seeing me for help was hopeless. Her response was, "Who wants help? I'm just here because nobody knows what to do with me and they want me off their back." She concluded every line of thought with the idea that everyone was deeply concerned by her behavior.

I asked the obvious question: "Do you think I'm worried about you?" She raged at me for the thirty minutes remaining in that hour and, with no added provocation on my part, continued to rage for the next three sessions. Emotionally, she expressed complete contempt for me. Intellectually, the substance of her thinking was that I was mercenary, cold, and "no goddamn good as a man."

Although the specifics of her arguments were distorted by her fury, I saw no reason to dispute the general thrust of her thinking. Relative to what she expected, I was cold, very cold. She was right in saying that I worked for money, and on several occasions I had made it clear that I would not see her if for any reasons, other than absolute necessity, she failed to pay her monthly bill in full and on time. As to my not being much of a man, she had every right to doubt my masculine prowess. I had never fought with her. I never urged her to talk when she was silent or tried very hard to slow her down when she talked too fast to be understood. I did not compare favorably with the men in her life with whom she had done battle. I did not protest these things because, given her frame of reference, they were true, and the one thing Becky needed was someone who would be true and absolutely honest with her from her frame of reference. Interestingly, all her thoughts and feelings about me were summed up with the words, "You don't care." Sometimes she screamed them and sometimes she whispered them, but it always meant the same thing: "I want you to care." I summed up my position with the words, "My caring is right behind yours. When you care about you, so will I."

A new element joined the struggle; the arguing and arrogance, the raging and petulant silences continued, but now she was also seductive. At first this was manifested in unexpected periods of cooperativeness in which she seemed reasonable, even docile. She assured me that she had met her match. Flattering as such a statement may have seemed, it demonstrated her complete misunderstanding of our work. It was a statement of capitulation to an enemy. Her behavior seemed better, but her suffering was no less; and it was, therefore, only a matter of time until her "good behavior" was also used as a weapon.

Becky's false pleasantness wore on. She began to wonder if there were really any reason for continuing.

Then she began to interpret small occurrences: for example, I saw her on the street and, contrary to her expectations, I said hello to her, as an indication that I was responsive to her new mood. Now she became openly sexually seductive. She talked in detail about her many group sexual experiences and elaborated all the ways she could please me. Eventually she convinced herself that my desire for her was so great that I could hardly stand to work with her. Although the means were different, her conclusion was the same; i.e., I could not stand her. When my lack of action proved to be a genuine lack of response rather than restraint, she was once again devastated. She was at her wit's end, because she had used all the means she had to alienate herself from me and she had failed. She could not get rid of me, but because I understood her illness, neither could I turn away from her. While closeness seemed impossible to her, rejection was unnecessary.

The approach dictated by the situation seemed cruel. I did in fact hurt Becky badly, but by the end of the first year of treatment, she was involved in a relationship that spoke to her needs and not society's demands; her pain and not her parents' embarrassment; her hopes and not my reputation.

Gradually her intense wish to be cared for became obvious, but it could not be openly admitted. Instead, she increased her efforts to convince me and herself that she was genuinely evil. Now, hours in which some degree of closeness was achieved were followed by actions she thought would necessitate my taking counteraction. When she was caught stealing from a local hardware store, she gave my name to the police in the hope that they would release her into my custody. She mishandled her job in a way that guaranteed discharge, but then told her boss to call me, in the hope that I would "make things all right for her." She saw my willingness to let her spend a weekend in jail and lose her job as sadistic rejection. Becky suffered. She wanted me to care but she demanded that I care for her as if she were an evil, impossible person. She insisted that my caring be in lieu of her own.

My refusal to handle the situations which she created was not a mere matter of analytic technique, nor was my unresponsiveness a rejection of her. It was only a rejection of the contrived picture she painted of herself in the hope of remaining unrevealed. If I had intervened in the trouble she created, both of us would have felt much better. The acts of talking to a desk sergeant at the police station or with an employer were small things. They would have given both of us that warm, inner assurance that I really cared and was willing to go the second mile. Becky would have felt better for a while. But she knew from her long experience that once she got people to "handle her" as a delinquent, it was only a matter of time until their patience would run out. Then they would leave her, lonely but still undisclosed.

There had to be a crisis. It happened on a beautiful spring morning. The bright warm weather seemed to intensify the depression and dread she felt in seeing me. She dropped her army surplus bag onto a chair across from me and then collapsed face down onto the couch. As her silence wore on, I noticed bugs—cockroaches—crawling out of her bag and spreading out over the chair. The situation was painful and obvious. She needed my undivided attention, but she knew that with bugs invading my office, I could only pretend to be attentive. To ignore the bugs would have been a repeat of the unrealistic, false acceptance she had experienced before, and Becky was poised to accuse me of pretense. Yet her condition that particular day was so desperate that interrupting the hour because of the cockroaches seemed irresponsible. Since I was sure Becky knew what was happening, I asked her to sit up and talk. Her response was, "You mean you want me to get the hell out of here!" She headed for the door and, almost certainly, a termination of her work with me. The bugs were fanning out on the floor. Action was called for. Becky reached the door and then turned back and asked if I really wanted her to leave. I suggested she sit down and help me decide what to do with the bugs.

We squashed the loose ones, but others kept crawling out of her bag. Examination of the contents of the bag revealed a rotting apple core, a used sanitary napkin, spilled cosmetics, contraceptives, and a billfold. Of course a simple solution to the bug problem was to take the bag to her car which was already contaminated, but that would have used up the remaining time, and then Becky and her problems would have been lost. We decided, therefore, to suspend the bag from a straight-back chair and put a metal wastebasket under it. Then we moved the entire contraption close enough to my chair so that I could kick occasionally and knock the emerging bugs into the basket. Becky lay down and for the first time poured out her true feelings; feelings of guilt and shame.

Our encounter with the bugs was momentous. It was the first time a relationship had proved trustworthy for Becky. It was trustworthy because she was not treated in terms of the trouble she caused or in terms of someone else's need to appear to be patient and caring. Becky was not rejected, nor was she merely tolerated. It was a trustworthy relationship because its goal was only to find out about Becky.

What we found was pervasive guilt—guilt so strong it almost possessed her. She was momentarily relieved to have it out in the open, but she was terrified when she felt the destructive power of the guilt we had uncovered. There was nothing intrinsically therapeutic about her expression of these painful emotions. Becky did not begin to improve simply because she had finally expressed her guilt. The honesty of our relationship had made it impossible for her to hide her real feelings behind a facade of arrogance, but bringing them into the open was not in itself curative. The only thing helpful about her expression of her "real" feelings was that it made possible an honest relationship with the real Becky.

An honest relationship was crucially important, because healing always evolves slowly as a result of a continuing relationship based on what one genuinely feels, thinks, and believes. Becky had never had such a relationship, because her life was devoted to the maintenance of an image which concealed her guilt. Doing away with the image forced her to see her real self and forced her to live with what she really felt about herself. It did not make her feel better. It made her feel much worse, but it was the beginning of a relationship in which change and healing could occur.

Becky's problems were intense and dramatic, but in some very important ways she was a prototype of many of today's disturbed young people. At heart, she was a young woman who felt deeply guilty, but her destructive behavior was not the cause of her guilt. Her behavior was a means by which she distracted herself and those who tried to help her from the pervasive guilt she felt over just being alive. Without understanding this, my ministrations as a physician would have been no more helpful to Becky than had been the patient efforts of her family. In order to begin a healing relationship with Becky, it was necessary to understand that arrogance and hostility, theft and sexual promiscuity are often simply means by which disturbed people draw attention away from a malignant sense of guilt about their own self.

Becky's family was religious, but they received no help from their church. Like so many churches, theirs had a fine tradition of concern for the guilt-ridden, but in practice, they were both unwilling and unprepared to deal with them. A few modern Christians still place the subject of guilt beyond any kind of investigation and understanding because they take for granted that a guilty conscience is the admonishing voice of God. From this frame of reference, it appears to be as irreverent to question the guilt-ridden conscience as it is to question the existence of God. It is difficult to determine what theological basis there is for this approach to guilt, but its net effect is to isolate those who live with guilt. Once segregated, men and women who struggle with relentless and demoralizing guilt occasionally disturb the main body of believers, but they are never accepted as a real part of it.

Psychologically knowledgeable Christians who are quick to sense the aura of illness which surrounds the lives of people consumed by feelings of guilt are often inadvertently rejecting when they automatically refer them to a therapist. This form of segregation is supported by various rationales such as that psychic trouble is for a doctor to deal with, or that the church is concerned with the spirit, not mental illness. There is some truth to these arguments, but the result of a too-cautious attitude toward the problem of guilt is that the modern church finds itself unable to speak to "sinners."

Christ's primary concern with sinners was beautifully described in his encounter with the Pharisees and scribes who saw him feasting with Levi and other tax collectors. They asked, "Why do you eat and drink with tax collectors and sinners?" And Jesus answered them, "It is not those who are well who need the doctor, but the sick. I have not come to call the virtuous, but sinners to repentance" (Luke 5:29-32, Jerusalem Bible). Christ never employed a loose analogy. He saw sickness in guilt and he made it clear that it was his concern to work with it. There is no reason to believe that Christ went about his work without understanding what he was up against. His success with people who resisted his efforts to help was not simply the result of good intentions and love. Obviously, Christ would have worked helpfully with Becky. The sincere but unknowledgeable efforts of Becky's parents are typical of contemporary Christians, but they are not typical of Christ.

This is not to suggest that views held by much of the secular world are better. One view which is growing among the ranks of dispassionate intellectualizers is that all guilt is essentially unhealthy and should be eradicated. Observation and study meant to enhance one's ability to help distressed people clearly demonstrate the function of guilt in the healthy mind. Debunking normal guilt is an invitation to the restrictions of mental turmoil. The notion that guiltless freedom is to be found in "doing your own thing" is simply false. It is a deception by which frightened people appear to be free while they are actually moving toward the immobilization of chaos.

To many people the pain of a pervasive sense of guilt is very real, but there is no more relief in moralizing than there is in rationalizing. People whose morality is grounded in religious faith often assume that it only makes sense for someone like Becky who has broken almost all the rules to experience guilt. In fact, religious people find guilt in these circumstances so appropriate that they often do not listen carefully. They fail to see the difference between a pervasive sense of guilt and guilt which follows an obvious moral transgression.

By a pervasive sense of guilt, I am referring to guilt which underlies every thought, feeling or deed; it challenges one's right to exist. Normal guilt, which is expected by us all, follows a violation of conscience. Pervasive guilt may drive its victim to wrongdoing, while normal guilt results from wrongdoing. Normal guilt is an uncomfortable tension which may become an unbearable burden. To escape it, one might attempt to deny the importance of the acts or thoughts which produced it. One might try to make restitution. A pervasive sense of guilt, however, is relieved, though temporarily, by the continued commission of punishable acts or the verbalization of reprehensible thoughts and feelings which act as a distraction.[2]

For example, the pervasive sense of guilt which controlled Becky's life did not result from her "bad" behavior.

---

[2] See Sigmund Freud, "Criminals Form a Sense of Guilt," in The Standard Edition of the *Complete Psychological Works*, ed. by James Strachey (London, 1957), vol. XIV, p. 332.

Actually she was relieved by her behavior because it always brought a response from others which enabled her to divert her attention away from her own feelings about herself. The system worked whether her parents punished her or forgave her. Either way, Becky's "bad acts" gave her relief from her underlying, pervasive sense of guilt for existing.

The kind of guilt we are describing is experienced as an agonizing conviction that one's self is essentially "bad." Characteristically, this guilt is vague and undefinable. It is different from guilt as it is commonly perceived, which is quite definite because it is a response to something thought or done. It is not guilt about being alive.[3] Sufferers of pervasive guilt angrily resist attempts to bring it into the open. They fear that if the curtain of confusion is parted and the "evil me" is revealed, life will be literally unbearable. Sometimes the bad self is experienced as an incessant, silent voice saying, "You're no good, you're no good." Attempts to laugh it off or challenge the voice only make it worse. Eventually the logical step is submission and perhaps suicide. Occasionally death is, in fact, resorted to, but much more often relief is gained by partial destruction in the prolonged death of depression.

Outright "sinfulness" like the use of drugs, antisocial acts, and inappropriate speech provide relief to someone like Becky. It is a relief to be in a coma; it is a relief to have something definite to feel bad about. It is a relief to be punished by someone else instead of by oneself. Being guilty for doing or saying something harmful or offensive

---

[3] See Sigmund Freud, "Criminals Form a Sense of Guilt," in The Standard Edition of the *Complete Psychological Works*, ed. by James Strachey (London, 1957), vol. XIV, p. 332.

is a relieving distraction. One need only say, "I'm sorry" and promise, "I won't do it again." Being guilty for being alive is something else. One cannot say, "I'm sorry and I won't exist."

Hence, the person who suffers from guilt of this kind is a paradox. His reprehensible actions are, in fact, his way of getting the tyrannical conscience within himself located outside himself. With his hurtful words and deeds the victim of pervasive guilt provokes people around him to react restrictively and punitively. Now his friends and family will say, "You're no good," and thus the voice of conscience is confirmed and externalized. Once outside oneself, the tyrant can be managed.

In order to illustrate the phenomenon of pervasive guilt, we have described it in an extreme form. When situations become acute, as they were for Becky, intensive professional help is a necessity. In a less intense form, however, such guilt is indeed very common. With courage and understanding the layman can be helpful, even when the problem is his own. But when the inner workings of guilt are not understood, one's best efforts are wasted on one reaction after another.

In the context of parental kindness, "spare the rod and spoil the child" is sometimes a realistic though incomplete guide to the management of discipline problems. It is a frame of reference within which generations of Christian people have grown up and within which they have raised their own children. Becky's problem appeared to be disciplinary, so it was quite natural for her well-intentioned religious parents sometimes to respond to it as if a firm hand were all that was really needed. But these efforts failed.

People using these kinds of distractions to deflect attention from their sense of guilt are troublesome to deal with. Concerned persons feel almost compelled to react in punitive terms to what appears to be deliberate and dangerous troublemaking. To be lenient not only seems to be inviting more serious trouble, it seems to be a failure to do one's duty. Of course, the angry reaction of indignant, self-righteous people is essentially selfish, and is, therefore, of no help whatsoever. However, one does not have to be selfish in order to feel constrained to react strongly; and in the case of arrogant youth, very strongly indeed.

People who suffer from a deep sense of personal guilt are not helped by even the most sincere admonitions. As we have seen, such people invite scoldings and lectures on morality. They are relieved by such reactions, but the problem still remains. Their sense of worthlessness increases. Despair and immobilization follow. This may look like laziness which calls for another punitive response, and thus a descending spiral is tightened.

Threats of punishment, if they are strong enough, may appear to inhibit the downward spiral for a while. Threats work because they powerfully focus the sufferer's attention on an external, identifiable person, and not on a voice from within. Even if one persists in threatening, eventually the fear produced will not be enough to drown out the sufferer's relentless inner conviction that he or she is "bad." Moreover, modern, charitable Christians have a great resistance to making frightening threats because the possibility of alienation from someone in trouble is unendurable.

Consider the effects of treating the problem liberally.

Suppose one decides to be nonjudgmental and allow as much freedom of expression as possible. In Becky's case this would have meant withholding judgment on expressions of gross immorality. This is not in the mainstream of the Christian tradition—a tradition supported by experience and ancient doctrine. There is, however, much in the scriptures that can be cited to support the idea of responding to conscience-stricken people with acceptance, which encourages openness rather than deception. Again, the problem is to recognize the conscience-stricken condition which lies beneath the troubled person's apparent disregard for morals and his inconsiderate treatment of others. Such an approach has promise only if the underlying sense of worthlessness is empathically understood. Only then can one's liberality be sincere.

A liberal attitude toward the expression of painful feelings of guilt must never imply an unrealistic permissiveness toward destructive action. Destructive action always decreases the chances for worthwhile talk. My work with Becky would not have improved if I had pretended not to care about the cockroaches. On the contrary, she would have known that I was insincere; and as a result, there would have been no relationship.

To be effective, one must remember that genuine acceptance deprives guilty people of the means by which they externalize their conscience, i.e., they are deprived of the punitive reactions which assist them in making their problem belong to others. It is very, very difficult for Christian people to realize that accepting love and patience is a deprivation to a guilty man or woman.

If the guilty person finds that the kindness with which he is treated is insincere, if it does not come from a real desire to understand the situation but is only meant to achieve an effect, he will exploit it until he is rejected and reinstated in the old ways. Patience in the sense of putting up with the problem will not endure the test. Patience which arises from an appreciation and understanding of the paradoxical nature of guilt can heal because it spares one the exhaustion of being constantly reactive to the provocations of the person with the problem.

If the situation is not too severe (and most commonly it is not), then eventually the sufferer will find it possible and helpful to begin to talk about his judgment of himself rather than the reactions of others. This is a frightening process which progresses slowly. At this point, the religious parent, spouse, or friend is apt to make a vital mistake. He is very tempted to remind the sufferer that God is a forgiving and accepting Father and that God is quick to forgive, no matter what kind of life one has led. Within the context of the believing community, this seems like a completely logical thing to say, but it is a mistake when one is working with a person who suffers from a sense of guilt over his own existence. Such a statement is helpful only if it clearly implies that because God accepts the worst in humankind, it is reasonable for humans to accept the worst in themselves. If one wishes to speak about the love of God, one must not imply that the love and acceptance of God can take the place of one's acceptance of oneself.

By the same token, the problem is not handled by forgiveness and absolution. Healing, whether physical or mental, must proceed from the inside and work toward the outside. Relief gained by the external applications of comforting words is like an old-fashioned poultice plaster for pneumonia. It warms the breast, but the infection grows worse. The sufferer must wrestle with guilt and accept the bad self. Then and only then can he or she find that in genuine acceptance even the "worst" elements in one's life can change.

That which is absolved, whether by priestly function, a layman's good will, or by a therapist's explanation, remains a separate "bad" part of oneself. No one else can take the place of self-acceptance based on a realization of what one is. Until then, the "bad" parts are separated from what one calls "me," and that which is separated cannot change any more than children locked in an attic room can mature. Like angry, frightened children, thoughts and feelings which are honestly accepted can be loved, and in love their natural development is re-established. Eventually, irrespective of their original malfunction, they can become valued members of one's psychic family. Growth and development is cultivated by a willingness to think, to feel, and to express. It thrives in the inclusiveness of understanding and acceptance.

The process of coming to realize that one's behavior is the result and not the cause of guilt proceeds slowly. It is slow because, as we have said, the guilt that produces a paradoxical effect is buried in the unconscious. It is always painfully intense and sometimes childish in nature, and so to own up to it is embarrassing. The understanding love of the helper must be present, but not declared in ordinary terms, and this is very hard for most Christians. As it was in my work with Becky, love is not so much a matter of sympathetic concern as it is a matter of honesty.

It may also be loving simply to wish to understand, to be hopeful, or to stay awake nights worrying, but this is not helpful love. To be helpful, one must realize that those who feel guilty falsify themselves in the hope of avoiding their guilt and the fear which guilt engenders. It is temporarily comforting but not loving to foster these deceptions because they make a genuine relationship impossible. Love between loved ones must be declared, but love with which one seeks to open a guilty mind must be silent. Until the process is complete, declarations of love are perceived by guilty persons as evidence that they are not understood; hence, the frequent cry of youth, "No one understands me." In spite of all the love that was declared to Becky, she never felt understood because she assumed that anyone who really understood what she was like would hate her as much as she hated herself. Of course, when one is guilty and afraid, it is a relief to be misunderstood, but it is also lonely because, irrespective of how much interaction there may be, there is no relationship, no hope of change.

Given the present state of our world, it is important for Christians to understand the sufferings of the guilty. There are large numbers of such people in our society, and reliable statistics show that a very large percentage turn to the church for help. Many, if not most, are young and talented. If Christian concern includes those among us who die slowly from the depression and despair that inevitably accompany pervasive guilt, then the church's need to understand the anatomy of guilt is urgent. Tragically, there is rarely anyone at church who senses that urgency.

Chapter 2

The Two Faces of Guilt

People who turn to the church out of a genuine need for help are one of the church's best hopes for a meaningful future as an agency of personal change. The pain caused by guilt in its various forms is often the major reason people seek help, but people suffering from a pervasive sense of guilt are always at cross purposes within themselves and cannot enter into the honest relationship they need. They search for closeness and then destroy it when it involves openness. Hence, it is essential that church people develop an understanding of guilt which goes far beyond sincere but uninformed caring. Becky's parents were Christian people who cared very much about their daughter, but they could not help her because they did not understand her; they did not know the facts.

Her parents did not realize that their love only highlighted Becky's sense of unworthiness; their patience only deprived her of the fights and arguments she used to distract and relieve herself from her unbearable sense of being evil. Only when these things were understood was Becky confronted with a relationship which she could not destroy or pervert; a relationship which offered her no opportunity to escape herself. Then, and only then, the guilt and self-hate that was her real problem poured out. Again, understanding was essential because the guilt which emerged threatened to overcome her wish to live.

She was shaken with fear. In a desperate bid for relief, Becky pleaded with me to hate her, to tell her she was no good and reject her, and thereby reestablish an external distraction from her internal problem.

Becky's terror in response to her confrontation with her guilt was not unique to her or to her generation. With new knowledge, people's insight into themselves increases but their basic reaction, their human nature, stays the same. People always flee from a revelation of their own judgment of themselves. Out of fear they try to separate themselves from relationships which cannot be distorted; which force them to face themselves. Consider the story of Simon Peter's first encounter with Christ.

And when he had ceased speaking, he said to Simon, "Put out into the deep and let down your nets for a catch." And Simon answered, "Master, we toiled all night and took nothing! But at your word I will let down the nets." And when they had done this, they enclosed a great shoal of fish; and as their nets were breaking, they beckoned to their partners in the other boat to come and help them. And they came and filled both the boats, so that they began to sink. But when Simon Peter saw it, he fell down at Jesus' knees, saying, "Depart from me, for I am a sinful man, O Lord." (Luke 5:4)

Peter was tired of fishing. He protested that he had caught nothing all night. But Christ would not be put off, and so Peter put out the nets and made the greatest catch of his life. Like any first-century man, Peter interpreted the catch of fish as a miracle and, like any first century man, he cared much less about the practical results of the miracle than he did about the meaning implicit in it. (Modern people would probably be mainly concerned about the catch.) Peter focused his attention on Christ, and so he sensed the revealing power of Christ which so many modern Christians miss. In Christ's presence, Peter was stuck with himself, and he was afraid.

The knowledge and insight of twenty centuries has changed people's interpretation of a great catch of fish, but it has not changed their reaction to a relationship which reveals their true nature. They are still afraid.

If, out of fear, Peter had simply wanted Christ to get out of his life, then he handled the situation very badly. All he really had to do was walk away. Instead, he fell down at Christ's knees, confessed his sinfulness, and then asked Christ to leave him. Like Becky, first he came wanting a relationship and then he asked for rejection. He yearned to be close, but he intuitively sensed the pain that was involved in closeness with a Man of power and honesty derived from testing and realization. So Peter tried to distort the relationship that had hardly begun. In falling down and saying, "Depart," Peter not only tried to deny his obvious wish to be close, but he also tried to make the whole affair Christ's decision, that is, Christ's problem.

Suppose Christ had departed because Peter was a "sinful man." Who would have ended up with the problem? Certainly not Peter, he would have thought. After all, he had admirably confessed his sinfulness. If Christ had left as Peter asked, Peter would have looked to himself like a good and honest man who had tried to be open but was only misunderstood. Christ would have looked to him like just one more miracle-worker, eager to show his power but not interested in standing behind his grand words. Christ would have been discredited and Peter—well, poor, rejected Peter would have been "off the hook."

Suppose Christ had accepted Peter on the basis of his confessed "sinfulness." If Peter's sinfulness were anything like the showy immorality with which Becky bedazzled and distracted people who frightened her, then accepting Peter on the basis of his sins would have been a grave error. It would have been the beginning of a false relationship doomed to superficiality and failure. Of course, Peter would have been relieved, but he would have remained just as lonely. Of course, Christ would have looked magnificent, but in fact he would have been party to a deception; he would have become a false prophet.

Suppose Peter were confessing that deep sense of wrong, of personal evil, which so frightened Becky when she was finally able to talk about it. Shouldn't Christ have offered forgiveness? Of course, according to Luke, Christ had not yet practiced the forgiveness of sins at the time of his initial encounter with Peter. Certainly, however, he was close to it. Christ's concern with forgiveness was demonstrated when, shortly after the Peter incident, he forgave the sins of a paralyzed man even before he healed the man of his paralysis. Why then did he not forgive Peter?

The question can undoubtedly be approached in several ways, but I would suggest that Christ withheld his forgiveness because, irrespective of the origin of Peter's guilt, he wanted to give Peter more than the transient relief of externally applied forgiveness. He wanted Peter to know the growth that could evolve only from a relationship in which Peter fully recognized and accepted himself. I suggest that he wanted to give Peter more because he saw that at heart Peter wanted more; he wanted to follow. Throughout Christ's ministry, men and women were joyously healed, forgiven, and then never heard of again.

Christ wanted to hear from Peter again, and so he withheld the forgiveness for which Peter asked.

Peter had no paralysis or demons to be cast out. He had no epilepsy to be healed. He had nothing to cushion his encounter with Christ but his sins, and so he gathered them up into a confession and interposed them between himself and Christ. But Christ withheld the warmth of forgiveness because Peter was meant to follow and grow to apostleship. He wished Peter to become the Rock of his church; the holder of the keys of the kingdom. Christ wished Peter to become all that he was capable of becoming, and so he did not offer relief. He offered and demanded relationship—relationship with the hidden man as well as with the obvious man.

Undoubtedly, Peter perceived what Christ really offered, but out of fear he denied his understanding and so Christ spoke to his fear. "And Jesus said to Simon, 'Do not be afraid; henceforth you will be catching men'" (Luke 5:10).

Christ did not admonish or forgive. He did not even speak to the sins which Peter brought up. Instead, he spoke to the fear which people always feel when they cannot escape from themselves. Like Becky, frightened people can find comfort in punishment and forgiveness, or in rebellion and destruction. But to grow, they must deal with their fear of facing themselves in the context of an enduring and honest relationship.

Christ's purpose was clear. He was interested in Peter becoming a catcher of men. He wanted to start Peter moving, so he spoke to the fear which people in the twentieth century, no less than people in the first century, must bear if their lives are to develop beyond the temporary pleasures of a child's game of naughty thoughts and actions, confessions of guilt and forgiveness. Moral "show and tell" has never fostered human development.

Christ wanted Peter out of fish and into people. He wanted Peter to speak with the same authority that characterized his own ministry. But Christ's authority was not a gift. It followed his struggle and temptation, his fearful wrestling with the easier alternatives open to him. Christ spoke to Peter's fear because he knew that if Peter were to reach beyond the narrow limits dictated by his fear of himself, he had to dare to be afraid. "Do not be afraid," did not circumvent Peter's problems; it only assured him that he was not alone with them. The months ahead were filled with conflict and despair, but in fear Peter was close to the Son of Man, and in growth he shared creation with the Creator.

A discussion of sacred scripture in which one draws parallels between the work of Christ and the work of a modern physician, and between the needs of a saint and the needs of a contemporary young woman is open to serious question if it is simply a comparison of the people involved. However, I do not mean to imply that Becky and I are comparable to Peter and Christ as persons. I mean only to suggest that the pain and conflict experienced by guilty people, whether CEO, street person or saint, must be resolved within the context of a scrupulously honest, accepting relationship.

A scholarly reader might question my discussion on the basis of modern evidence which suggests that the Lucan account of Christ's calling of Peter is an amalgamation of several pieces of information which were not originally connected. The Bible may not be an accurate recording of historical events, as current scholarship maintains, but it is never mere invention. It never circumvents the fundamental realities of human reaction as they were observed and experienced by the writers. I have not chosen to expound upon the Lucan text because it is more or less historically accurate than similar passages in Matthew or Mark. Luke's account clearly differentiates Christ's dealing with the problem of guilt in a man whom he hoped would grow to apostleship from his handling of people who were satisfied with miraculous relief.

The layperson might object to the complexity of the interpretation I have made of this simple event. I agree that elaborate hypotheses built on a few scant facts are often more academically fascinating than insightful. My interpretation, however, is based not only on the event under discussion, but also on our knowledge of the life of Peter and Christ after they met.

Legitimate questions about the analytic parallels I have drawn cannot be overlooked, but I hope they will not obscure consideration of my conclusions. I conclude that Peter, like Becky, was conflicted. His problems became intensified and unavoidable in the searching relationship which Christ offered. Christ recognized the storm that raged within Peter, because he himself had only recently been through a period of conflict. I conclude that the disturbing, fearless authority with which Christ spoke after his trial in the desert cannot be dismissed simply as a supernatural gift that has little implication for the modern reader. Christ's authority was a natural result of his recognition and acceptance of the conflicting forces within himself. It was a result of growth predicated on facing the inner truth of his own life.

The modern church member, however, seldom believes that his religious life should lead him into personal conflict. Of course Christian people do a lot of worrying. But mostly they worry about thinking, speaking, and acting in ways which help them avoid the conflicting facts of their personal life. Unlike Christ, many present-day Christians do not wish to see that there is more hope of real change in the conflict aroused by sinfulness that is honestly faced, than there is in pretended righteousness. To this end, these Christians place Christ on a pedestal and quietly assume that he was divinely and placidly beyond the torment of honest people. We talk about Christ having borne the burdens of humankind, but the unspoken assumption behind such talk is that in his divinity he was never at his wits' end; he never despaired. So also the saints are venerated as cool characters who always did "their thing" the "right way." In fact, however, the bewildering insights Christ thrust upon those who chose to follow him constantly exposed them to their true motivations and led to personal struggle.

Christ on a pedestal is comfortable and not at all like the Christ who spoke with unchallengeable authority to Peter. The Christ of history spoke with authority that came from an ongoing process of self-examination, acceptance, and change. The stagnant authority of "good people" who invoke the faith in justification of their self-righteousness, but do not participate in Christ-like struggles, open the church to attack from detractors of the faith. These detractors are all too willing to unmask the selfishness and anger that lie behind such self-righteousness and the pleasure that so often motivates punishment. But Christ's authority was the authority of a Man who knew what he was made of, because he had looked at himself, struggled with himself, and found acceptance. He was never caught off guard by the cunning Pharisees because he was never on guard. Christ could never be manipulated by the threat of an exposé because he knew what humankind was and he had faced himself as a human being.

The emasculated voice with which this part of the modern church speaks does not reflect the potent truth portrayed by its ancient Lord. It cannot offer the revealing relationship which characterized the life of Christ because it does not confront men and women with the revealing facts of human life from which personal conflict arises; conflict from which individual and collective authority emerges. Instead, the church clings to the benign vestiges of the virulent power it once knew by virtue of its ability to make people afraid, ashamed and guilty. As a consequence, many Christians turn away from the dynamic, revealing authority of Christ and hold, instead, to the passive confidence that can be derived from a mindless and convenient obedience to a patchwork quilt of "good behavior."

In some churches, life that is comfortably cramped and circumscribed, life that is safely limited by a dread of knowing, can still be lived under the comforting aegis of unquestioned authority. But full life in today's world is far too complex for such comfort. Enough rules cannot be invented to cover the exigencies of a single day. The modern church can never recreate the power base from which it has spoken for centuries. Today the authority of the church must come from the collective authority of individuals who have found in the Christian faith a basis for an ongoing process of unfolding awareness and personal discovery, followed by new strength and commitment. Only authority based on the dynamic change of individuals has the resilience to move and grow with our changing world. Only authority which arises from personal experience is both firm and credible.

When Christ spoke to Peter's fear rather than to his sin, he did not disavow the authority of the commandments. He simply superseded that authority with faith in the ability of those who are faced with facts to reaffirm God's ancient truth in terms that speak authoritatively to their own existence. The authority which is distinctly Christian arises from the ability of human beings to search, doubt, and wrestle within themselves, and thereby grow toward responsibility.

Because modern Christians see Christ's relationship with the apostles in unreal terms, "conflict" and "struggle" are almost un-Christian words. Christians seem convinced that the anxiety of our age is an extraordinary burden and that the fruits of religion should be relief. So far as growth is concerned, relief, in the sense of freedom from anxiety, is no more available to honest people of our time than it was to honest people of the past. However, struggle engaged in under the aegis of the Christian faith does indeed relieve the loneliness of self-righteousness and the isolation of life. In the Christian life, struggle is not hopeless turmoil. It is a painful but fruitful personal search in the companionship of men and women of honest concern and love. In the Christian life, personal struggle and insight that is initiated by a relationship with Christ is always intimately related to the lives of others. Human motives are common denominators of human existence and, therefore, no matter how righteous they may appear, those who dare not look honestly at their own motives miss the real basis for Christian relationship.

It is vitally important to differentiate between facing one's true motives and developing an honest relationship in which one's motivation can change and grow. Christ understood the basic facts of human nature. With his understanding, he might have attracted a following of like-minded individuals. But Christ wanted change—fundamental change such as eventually characterized the lives of his followers. But change cannot come from a mere understanding of facts alone. Knowledge changes people's ideas but not people. For example, Becky's parents could not help her because they did not understand her, but by the same token she was not helped by me simply because I did understand her. She was helped because my understanding made a relationship of trust and caring possible. Hence, growth for modern Christians is not only a matter of responding once again to the revealing, conflict-provoking authority of Christ. Growth also depends on a relationship. Christ revealed Peter to himself, but he did not leave him alone.

Today many men and women of knowledge question the necessity of the existence of the church. The same people are magnetically attracted to the many "new" theories of psychotherapy which are abroad. Tragically, such people do not realize that today's new theories are as unable to assuage guilt, conquer fear, dissolve hate, and move people toward love as was yesterday's religious mysticism. When any theory is not the basis of a continuing and responsible relationship of sincere concern, it fails to help. Today's guilty, frightened, hurt people are not better off because they can explain their pain in terms of brilliant psychological theories. By the same token, yesterday's glorious religious revelations did not change people, but only quieted their anxiety.

And so, irrespective of the promising movement of the modern church toward getting people to open up and reveal themselves, its usefulness as a means by which the lives of troubled people are transformed still depends on its existence as a community of caring men and women. Sincere concern cannot be implemented without accurate knowledge, but knowledge without relationship is profound futility.

Insofar as clergy and laity are convinced that the future of the church depends on their cautious handling of each other's private beliefs and idiosyncrasies, there is no Christian community. As we have seen in the life of Becky and the life of Peter, fact-facing alone does not bring relief. It may make one feel worse. But Christians have a right and a duty to profess a faith that dispels the comforting illusions of life even at a time when people clamor for relief, because people also yearn to grow away from guilt toward affirmation and love. To love one's neighbor as oneself is not just an illusory goal; it is a shared reality between men and women who accept the wholeness of each other because they have faced the two faces of themselves.

Chapter 3

"God, I'm Being Born"

Becky gradually dropped the destructive means by which she had avoided facing her guilt. She expressed her feelings more and more freely. Unfortunately, we soon reached a stage in which talk about guilt took the place of expressions of guilt. The talk became incessant and the subject matter petty. It expressed no conflict, no hard thinking, and no meaningful change. In sharp contrast to the pain Becky had experienced in previous sessions, which had been filled with emotions and ideas, she was now quite comfortable. The more she talked, the more comfortable she became. We were stuck in a mire of talk.

It became clear that Becky had assumed that her glib thinking about guilt was fascinating to me. Having assumed this, it was easy and natural for her to further assume that the understanding of the subject matter which I demonstrated reflected satisfaction with myself and with her. Again she had managed to get her problems outside herself. She knew that she felt better when I was "understanding" her. Therefore, her goal became to please me and keep the comfort flowing. That no permanent change had occurred within Becky became obvious when I was out a few days with the flu. She became frantic. All the old fears came back.

Becky's feeling of closeness to me was precious to her. She had rarely known the security of a reliable relationship. She felt much better, but unfortunately her relationship was now based on the mistaken notion that her salvation lay in her pleasing me, thus assuring my continued interest.

Her hours with her "shrink" had become the only times in the week when she felt she could put her head together and feel "right." She laughed nervously when it occurred to her that the comfort she felt with me was the kind of thing her mother had expressed in her often-quoted phrase, "Honey, just live every hour with Jesus." To Becky's mother, Jesus was "instant comfort." All one had to do was please him. I had become Becky's comforter. At one time, guilt had been an agonizing reality that had to be uncovered and expressed. Now it was merely a topic which Becky used in the hope of getting me to support and reassure her. It was a means by which she made me look bigger than life and singularly concerned with her. Things were much better but only because Becky was pathetically deluded. She had not solved her problems. She had just imagined me to be a magical problem solver.

Becky's family and friends became aware of her attachment to me, because she insisted on imitating me, that is, on "analyzing" everything and everybody. Every family argument had to be "thought through" and the "real motives discovered." She insisted on bringing "insight" to people whether they wanted it or not. She endlessly exposed her thoughts and feelings of guilt; and if others did not follow her lead, she suspected they were too guilty to talk.

There had been a time when Becky's family was deeply hurt by the delinquency which separated her from them. In those days when the strain of separation became unbearable, Becky would do something particularly "bad." Then there would be a blow-up followed by statements of regret and promises to do better. The reunions thus effected rekindled warmth and hope in the family and friends, but not in Becky. Eventually their "goddamn kindness" was too much for her. Dad would slip her a few dollars on the side for some new clothes; he would pointedly refrain from commenting on the blue jeans she had worn without washing for three weeks. Mother would carry on about the "really attractive features" she had discovered in Becky's boyfriend; she would pointedly avoid mentioning her abhorrence, obvious to Becky, of a boy who "never took a bath," wore shoulder-length hair, and took pleasure in a vocabulary limited to "baby," "wow," "cool" and "man." To Becky, separation was bad, but these false attempts to achieve closeness were even more painful. They reminded her of how fake she really was and how superficial her moments of peace at home were. And so, she would "split."

But now things at home were entirely different. Before, the family had been pained by Becky's isolation. Now, they could hardly stand her closeness. There were no blow-ups and subsequent reunions. Instead, the family was quizzed, grilled, exposed, defined and explained until they were totally on the defensive. Becky thought this was a "beautiful," a "really beautiful," solution for every difficulty. She insisted that any wish for privacy in the family was an indication of guilt, of a desire to keep something secret because of guilt.

Disturbing as Becky's new behavior was to the family, they could not deny that she was improved.

(Sometimes Becky was disturbing because she made a pest of herself, but often she was just too accurate and revealing for comfort.) She was not the "good girl" they had hoped for, but she was sleeping at home now. She went to school, took baths (with the bathroom door open), and much of the time she dressed in ways which approached the family's standards for girls. They were both disturbed and pleased. Becky was obviously much improved, but the relentlessness with which she pursued the subject of guilt gripped them. She was everywhere. Even when she was not present, they were aware of her ideas and felt obliged to question their motives. To do otherwise seemed like a rejection of Becky just when she was being restored to them.

Christians are often painfully befuddled by this kind of improvement in a troublesome loved one. Quite naturally they assume that the apparent change which has been achieved is in response to their prayers, their loving desire to forgive and forget, to be understanding and to set an example. All the evidence points in that direction. In thought, word and deed there is obvious improvement. Seeing things this way, Christians redouble their efforts. But the troubled person only responds with more demands for "understanding," and more fault-finding with and analysis of the helpers.

After enough of this, the religious person dealing with someone like Becky eventually feels exhausted, then used, and finally sick and tired of the relentless scrutiny and "helpfulness."

People from a religious background feel obliged to be endlessly patient and forgiving in the face of difficulties like Becky presents, especially when she seems to be making genuine progress. However, when she continues to challenge and turn the helpers' helpfulness against them by endlessly criticizing and doubting their sincerity, they inevitably succumb to frustration. Then rejection of the sufferer is only a matter of time, and all for the wrong reasons.

Compulsive confessions of guilt are not as important in their content as in their function. People who suffer with a chronic sense of isolation, whether from guilt or from some other cause, find that scrupulous and repetitive confessions of guilt over faults and shortcomings command attention from well-meaning Christians. But the person used as an absolver of guilt does much more than is apparent. In a very real way, he or she takes over such a person's life and, in turn, is taken over by them. Because the helper appears to accept responsibility for another's life, he or she does not absolve guilt as much as relieve the anxiety of being a separate individual. Guilt for people like Becky has a continuing function. It spares them the pain and frustration that inevitably accompanies foreclosing on the hopes, joys, and innocence of childhood. In other words, people who use endless professions of guilt as a means of maintaining a relationship of comfortable dependency experience growth as a rejection, as a painful separation. More importantly, they see the Christian faith as a means of remaining a child forever.

This is a crucial insight, but it is difficult for Christian people to grasp. If one wishes to be helpful, one must see how persons who yearn for closeness cling to guilt, because in the repetitive relief of forgiveness, one can feel nurtured. In this way one's life is embraced and supported by the strength of others. This is the way Becky came to use her guilt. The expression of guilt became a technique for achieving a feeling of closeness to me built on the illusion that she was giving me what I wanted. Of course, Becky was incorrect. Expressions of guilt were not what I wanted and giving me what I wanted was not really a way of being close to me or accomplishing her purpose in therapy. Church people often feel that they are being helpful when they listen patiently to such endless confessions, but not understanding how guilt works, they are really not achieving closeness but simply fostering continued dependency.

Church people cannot help without understanding, but they are not free to understand unless they are willing to examine critically their church's long-term investment in providing this limiting form of comfort. Lonely people, who have only their guilt to keep them warm, legitimately turn to the church for comfort. Incongruously, if their concern for their sins is endless and trivial, the church will offer the illusory comfort of endless listening and reassurance. But if the chronically penitent begins to chafe at the confines of a relationship maintained by guilt, if they dare bear the discomfort of understanding what they are doing, they may find that the Christian, whether clergy or lay, may be unable to move on with them into a more mature relationship. The modern church can be a lonely place for those who wish to share the discomfort of growth. Growth requires a continuing relationship in which, despite discomforts, it is safe to search, to learn, and to change.

Becky's high regard for me began to grow into admiration and then love. In Becky's eyes, I could do no wrong.

I was everything she had ever wanted. At times she wished for me to be her lover. She insisted that only my concern for my professional reputation held me back from making her my "one and only favorite." Other times she saw me as a kind of loving father anxious to help her.

But more and more she experienced me through the eyes of a frightened infant yearning to be held and cared for. Since Becky's trouble began in childhood, it was completely natural for her to want to re-create and live through the early experiences of her life. The more she expressed herself, the more faith she developed in our relationship and the more faith she had, the more she was drawn toward the long-forgotten experiences of infancy.

The emerging feelings of childhood—the wishes, the frustrations, and the injustice—were embarrassing and painful, but even more difficult for her to tolerate was the emergence of an infantile frame of reference. That is, Becky not only experienced childlike feelings, but also began to view the world, and particularly her relationship with me, with the simplicity and naïveté of a child. It was humiliating for her. Like a lonely child, she yearned to be loved. Her weekends, when there were no therapy sessions, were filled with a sense of isolation that was tolerable only because she constantly daydreamed. But her hope for childish gratification as well as her hope for genuine help urged her into a deeper relationship with me. At the same time, however, the anxiety and pain which was always involved because she did not get the response she wanted from me, caused her to hold back. Most of the time she moved along, but she was never free of conflict.

Her incessant talking was a thing of the past. The relationship which had started when we spoke to the guilt and fear that lay behind her wild behavior had stood the test of her talkative efforts to imitate me, and now it was deepened by her courageous sharing of her most intimate and fragile self. The more she entrusted herself to me, the more important I became to her, and as she found me willing to bear the responsibility for fostering her emerging maturity that went with being centrally important to her, she trusted me even more. She was moving.

It is probably clear by now that Becky had an unusual capacity to express herself. Her ability became more pronounced as she struggled to express the memories, ideas, and feelings which accompanied the psychologically regressed (i.e., childlike) state of mind that now filled her therapy hours. But increasingly she found herself using the phrase "as if" to preface a description of something she felt. Becky was not hedging or losing her ability to express herself. She was trying to communicate her re-experiencing of vague but powerful feelings which had been felt originally in babyhood, that is, before she had words with which to express them. These were feelings which had never been expressed with words. They had been expressed in the primitive language of infancy: crying, kicking, sucking, cooing, etc. Sometimes she could express the feelings more accurately if she spoke poetically or used analogy or fantasy. More and more, ordinary adult language became an inadequate vehicle for expressing the nebulous but consuming emotions of infancy.

Slowly the frightening and humiliating, the blissful and hopeful experiences and emotions of childhood came alive. Slowly she came to know each one, and as she came to know it, the fear and pain associated with it were dissolved. She was winning her right to range freely throughout her mind without fear of what she might discover; without having to avoid elemental parts of herself.

Her hours were filled with a sense of weakness, but, painful as her work was, she was not so alone now. All of Becky's life had been spent trying to be close to someone bigger than herself; someone whose understanding would transcend her infantile dread and hatred of herself. She came to realize that she had never felt "really born"; she had never felt that someone had labored to give her life. She was just "a happening."

On questioning, her parents confessed that they had always loved her, but at the time of her birth they had been married only four months. They loved her but she was a source of fear and guilt to them. They could not be strong for her. Consider the position of an infant girl born into a family that is embarrassed and even ashamed of her presence. She could not be told, "Don't worry, this has nothing to do with you. It's all a matter of your parents' immature fears and worries." Becky could only sense the tenseness with which she was held. She could not comprehend, but she felt the coldness with which she was treated whenever the strange faces of guests appeared in the house. She felt the difference between the occasional nursing she received and her usual feeding via a bottle propped up on a pillow.

In the infantile state, Becky, like every child, was obliged to experience everything in terms of herself. Therefore, since the predominant feeling in her infancy was isolation, she could only develop the sense that there was something wrong with her. Her efforts to be good and earn closeness had to fail, because the trouble was not with her. The trouble was with the frightened parents whose ambivalence about her laid the basis for her "bad" evaluation of herself. When her persistent efforts to be close to them failed, despair and then rebellion followed.

Becky was pained by the emergence of her underlying feelings, but as she came to realize how mistaken her original judgments of herself had been, she began to allow a whole new person to be brought to light. For years she had not dared reveal her true identity to others or to herself. Now the emergence of old ideas, feelings, memories, wishes, and concepts began to fit together. Becky began to feel like a person. She began to feel like someone who had been a baby, a child, an adolescent. She felt depth. In her pain and struggle, she moved toward new recognitions and acceptance and then to a deeply gratifying realization of wholeness. Again, the feeling was too basic and too intense to be communicated accurately. She said only, "God, I'm being born."

Certainly these words have a familiar ring to Christian people. Hope of new birth has been a central concern of the faith since Christ first spoke to Nicodemus. Perhaps because it is so central, many devoted Christians react uneasily if not negatively to any attempt to relate this phenomenon of faith to psychological and scientific investigation. Much of the time this resistance to investigation is predicated on the fear that faith which is investigated is automatically robbed of its transcendent, supernatural quality.

In matters which are peripheral to faith, this apprehension is no longer a problem. For example, except in isolated instances, most Christians no longer believe that their faith is diminished because they turn to scientific medicine rather than rely on faith healing for the treatment of physical disease. But an objective discussion of something so basic as rebirth, which is fundamental, qualitative change, may still appear to some Christians as an attempt to explain away the majesty and power of faith. On reflection, however, we realize that understanding does not necessarily destroy but probably deepens faith. Understanding does, however, make untenable the fantasy that the results of faith are special rewards to the faithful. The good and natural results of faith are never injured by new facts, ideas, and understanding. Only the illusion that one earns and deserves those results is lost if one dares to add greater understanding to one's faith.

Understanding the rebirth of Becky does not take the magic out of it. Her experience of being born was the natural end result of her reliving and accepting previously denied aspects of herself. The whole process seemed strange to her, only because she had never had a relationship in which it was possible for her to reveal herself.

For people with a secure Christian faith, there is always such a relationship available in Christ. We always have, in him, the accepting parent, the understanding companion. Then, reliving parts of childhood and seeing the world once again through the eyes of a child is a common, natural, and revitalizing experience.

One of the greatest advantages of a game of touch football is that one feels like, and for a while becomes, a kid again. More importantly, in the act of sexual love there is a kind of regression, that is, a recapitulation of infancy. We, in part, fall back to the frame of reference of an infant from which he or she who satisfies us is all-power and all-beauty. For a moment we forget the limitations of present-day reality and we enjoy a satisfaction which is comparable in its intensity and its completeness to a child satiated at the breast.

Unfortunately, many modern Christians have become so intellectualized and/or pragmatic that regressive experiences are largely excluded from their religious life. But regression is a fact of life and believers cannot lay it aside without running the risk of having their beliefs replaced by theories and their convictions by dogma. The exciting advances in biblical scholarship and theology of recent decades have fostered the development of sound arguments which support the idea that everyday regressive events, from football to lovemaking, are essentially religious in nature. However questionable the theology of such arguments may seem to the person in the pew, they offer some much needed help to Christians to whom "religion" is restricted to churchgoing, morality, and a mechanical profession of faith.

Unhappily, the thoughtful Christian to whom a theology of regression has meaning often assumes that the appropriate result of a religious experience is simply a feeling of rejuvenation. "Letting it all hang out" is undeniably a good and pleasurable experience, particularly to Christians who habitually equate religion with "keeping it all hung up." Refreshing and helpful as such experiences are, however, they appear shallow when compared to Christ's concept of being born anew.

Consider Christ's declaration to Nicodemus: "Truly, truly, I say to you, unless one is born anew, he cannot see the kingdom of God." Nicodemus had trouble with Christ's assertion even though he was quite familiar with the ritual of being born into the community of believers at baptism. The Gospel of John pictures Nicodemus taking Christ literally, and, taken literally, the idea of rebirth is nonsense, even coming from a worker of miracles. Modern symbolic interpretations usually open the door to generalizations and easy applications, but in this instance Christ's symbolism is too specific and too powerful to be interpreted either generally or superficially. He was not referring to the good, healthy experiences of life which make one feel young again. Neither was he referring to the insights and revelations which so often accompany life's precious mystical moments. He had in mind the birth of a new person, a person qualitatively changed.

Christians of all ages and of all sects have tried to tone down Christ's unequivocal declaration. A traditional way of doing this is to subsume the entire concept of new life unobtrusively in the much more nebulous phrase, "a child of God." In this way the dynamism of rebirth is comfortably lost in a sea of generalized and questionable sentimentality. In modern Christian parlance, "a child of God" rarely connotes either the curiosity, discovery and growth characteristic of children or the searching struggles of the men and women of the Old Testament to whom the appellation originally applied. On the contrary, when applied to the modern Christian's personal life, the phrase is used to justify a passive and naïve approach to reality. When applied to the Christian's interpersonal life, it supplies a rationale for treating one's fellow human being "as if" he were a brother (but without the conflicts of real-life brothers!).

Being a child once again, being born anew, is not a convenient concept with which one can puree the stuff of life. It is not a psychological theory with which one can give a sophisticated rationale to "brotherhood." It is a living possibility.

When Becky cried, "God, I'm being born," the possibility of a new life was realized. This is not to suggest that successful psychoanalytic work makes Christians out of patients. It most decidedly does not. The point is that Christ talked of fundamental change which prepared one for entrance into a new life. Human change (so basic that it deserves the phrase "born anew") is a natural result of a psychological regression that goes beyond the recapturing of pleasant childhood activities and feelings. In rebirth, that which fear and rejection once forced one to lock up in the closets of the mind is brought out into the light of awareness. The result is joyous wholeness, but the process is always painful. That which was put away out of pain and fear is always frightening and painful to bring out.

Christ's preoccupation with the natural processes of growth was not simply a matter of getting his message across to his agrarian listeners. The parables with which he tried to portray the changes that must be wrought in his followers dealt with seeds and growing, leaven and fermenting, birth and newness, because only these elemental substances and events of life transcended the awe-inspiring, crowd-gathering results of his miracles.[4] Given a first-century frame of reference, Christ's healings and exorcisms were genuine. But Christ was not distinguished by his miracles. There were many miracle workers in his day. Christ was and is distinguished because he went beyond his miracles and showed men and women the

---

[4] See C. H. Dodd, *The Parables of the Kingdom* (New York, 1961; rev. ed.), p. 10

fullness of life. People were frightened at the idea of becoming something new. They were terrified at the idea that becoming something new was a present possibility. That the process involved owning up to one's hidden motives, childish wishes, and secret hopes; that it involved abandoning all pretense of goodness in favor of an acceptance of reality was more painful than most people could bear. But rediscovery of the whole person, rebirth of the hidden self, could happen and can happen no other way.

The distinguishing features of Becky's rebirth were the development of a relationship with me based on the whole truth and the pain, fear, and frustration she had to face within that relationship. Her new birth was in no way simply a pleasurable "new lease on life," but in her agony she came to realize that she was accepted and understood. To Becky this was love more powerful than she could comprehend. The uplift, even the glorious feeling of perspective and understanding that may accompany the revealing events of everyday life, is quite natural but very different from the anxiety that inevitably accompanies new birth. To bring forth a new person, Becky had to allow herself to be involved in a frighteningly powerful relationship in which she re-experienced the infantile roots of her life. The more awareness she gained, the more she relied on me and the more awesome I became. Becky was free to decide for or against continued involvement in the process, but she was not free to control the unfolding process. The relationship and the new growth it cultivated were awesome and frightening; but as she discovered and accepted the previously forgotten and rejected aspects of herself, she became dramatically aware of becoming a new person, someone she had never known before. However pleasing the results, the process was painful. But as she grew to trust me and herself, as she surrendered herself to a fuller admission of all that she was, she experienced genuine change because, when accepted, that which was "bad" began to grow and develop until it was "good" and lovable.

Since there is so much talk these days about the virtue of communication and acceptance I want to be explicit about the growth of "bad" things into things that are "good and lovable." Robert, a depressed, passive man, discovered that he was full of rage. If he blew up at someone, he would feel guilty and retreat into quiet passivity. If he blew up at someone who said, "That's okay, you haven't hurt me and I'm glad you got it off your chest," he may have felt great relief for a while. When he blew up within the therapeutic relationship, where those reassuring responses which would allow him to focus his attention on the effect of his anger on someone else were not forthcoming, then he began to ask himself, "What is this anger about?" It turned out that he really thought his anger was childish, but not bad. Now an interesting thing happened. Once the anger was genuinely accepted by Robert himself, it began to change. The more he accepted it the less boisterous and uncontrollable it became. Gradually Robert's anger became a constructive force in his life. His anger matured. It grew, just as a child who is accepted and loved will grow. Robert's anger was repressed and set aside years before when it was boyish anger. If it was to grow it had to be accepted as boyish anger, but in acceptance change occurred. Robert began therapy passive and depressed. He ended active and accepting of himself. That is change. Insight is not good enough. The assurances of others are not good enough. Acceptance within a continuing relationship which denies reassurance (it's usually false anyway) and thereby brings the sufferer to an awareness of his need to evaluate and accept himself—this brings change.

If the personal, qualitative change to which Christ so often referred is indeed a mystical gift granted to the naïve in reward for their unquestioning willingness to believe the leader, then there is nothing to talk about and no question to ask. Christ did not say, "Believe everything I tell you and you will be rewarded." He said, "Believe in me." The statement is a clear demand for relationship. He knew his people, and particularly he knew the apostles. There is very little evidence that he gave any of them much reassurance. "Before the cock crows, you will deny me three times" is not a reassuring statement. As a result, the apostles eventually went through the agony of self-recognition, and they did change.

Where in all Christendom is there a clergyperson who, while listening because he needs to understand, will refrain from giving the usual reassurances? The person whom he wishes to help will never appraise and accept himself as long as he is offered the comforting evaluation of others. It is my experience that clergy and Christians in general usually don't listen to each other as much as they might, and when they do, it is in order to provide an opportunity to be a comforting "good person." These Christians don't change very much.

Analysis did not make Becky a Christian, but insofar as she was involved in this process of elemental change, she shared rebirth with Christians to whom faith means constantly becoming "a new creature." Few people are granted the ability or have the need for an experience as deep and as profoundly changing as was Becky's. But within the context of a faith in which people are obliged to grow as a natural response to the accepting love of God, everyday life affords opportunities to see oneself more honestly, accept oneself more fully, and enjoy new wholeness.

A very aggressive young man named Andy suddenly developed ominous neurological symptoms. The situation was tense. His doctor feared that his condition was fatal, but definitive tests took several weeks to complete. Andy was completely confident he could stand the strain of waiting and so he was dismayed when he found himself becoming more and more childish in his wishes and behavior. As the number of sleepless nights mounted, he began to see the world through the eyes of a beseeching, frightened child. He was angry and embarrassed to find himself looking forward to church and communion as if "I was really going to be fed." Fortunately he shared his feelings with the friends with whom he usually had breakfast after the early morning communion. He did that in the hope that someone would tell him he was acting like a kid; tell him to "cut it out and grow up." Instead, a friend said, "Of course you feel like a kid. You're scared out of your head." Another man said, "You've always been so capable, so on top of everything; maybe now you're going to see what it's like to be human." But a third man, a young priest, said, "Maybe now you're going to find out what it's like to be a Christian —it's always been this way with Christians who really live the life. They go through everything with such blasted honesty that half the time they feel like scared kids. But because they don't fool themselves, they manage to know that they are accepted. Somehow they come out of these things stronger, not drained; more complete, not all divided up into logic-tight compartments by a bunch of rationalizations." Andy didn't feel very comforted by this conversation, but he knew he had the best kind of support there was.

By the time the tests were completed and Andy learned that his condition was a temporary problem that could be cured, he was a very different man. In his anxiety, he had experienced the fear and loneliness of childhood, but because he shared himself with Christian friends who had much more to offer than comfort, he learned. He accepted an element in himself he had not known existed. He emerged a man of greater kindness, a man much less afraid of being afraid. He was no less aggressive, but now he was strong.

The overriding, tragic irony of the modern church is that honest, searching men and women find more possibility of real change outside its structure than within it. The church's theologically indefensible emphasis on fixated stability drives such people away. But actually a genuine Christian theology is alive, and it is meant to keep its believers alive and moving. The idea of freeze-drying certain attitudes and concepts, laudable in themselves, is a distortion of the faith. So also is the notion that Christians are stronger when they attempt to exclude undesirable thoughts and feelings. This exclusion not only contradicts the words and actions of Christ, it is an invitation to depression and perhaps even suicide. Most often, people who think only "desirable" thoughts are merely people capable of deceiving themselves. When the church embraces and encourages this kind of thinking, it inherits the emotionally segregated—those persons cut off from their true motivation, dead persons.

An ongoing process of individual rebirth depends on the availability of an utterly accepting relationship and a personal willingness to bear the anxiety which inevitably accompanies an inward search. Becky's achievement was not the result of steeling herself against the thoughts and impulses that threatened to ruin her. She moved toward new life because she examined herself within a relationship which was predicated on an inclusion of every aspect of her past and present life. Nothing was excluded because it was "bad," embarrassing, or frightening. I do not suggest that there was or is something intrinsically good about expressing such thoughts; and I am certainly not saying that Becky's emotions were good or "beautiful" simply because they were expressed with sincerity and courage. I wish only to emphasize the fundamental fact that no change can occur in any element of one's personality that one does not fully accept. One cannot change that which one disavows.

Becky's growth and change occurred only in the full light of awareness. Only then could she experience acceptance for all that she was, rather than rejection for failing to be what she "should be." Only then could she realize that childhood rejection and childish hatred could grow and change when genuinely accepted. Obviously this is a long step beyond the simple erection of moral or aesthetic barriers to the recognition of disquieting elements in oneself. It is a step which requires that the people involved stay and work with their relationship even though that relationship is characterized by anxiety, fear, and embarrassment.

This is an impossible task if one believes that new birth is simply a reward for righteousness. Birth, whether physical or mental, is truly miraculous, but it involves continuing tension and pain as well as the joy of new life. Unfortunately, many Christians see tension and anxiety as a sure sign that there is something wrong with their religious life. Contrary to the life of Christ, the history of the church, and the most fundamental precepts of Christian theology, Christians fail to understand that the serenity of new wholeness involves the struggle of new birth. The avoidance of pain and anxiety is not exclusively Christian; it is human. It becomes a special fault for Christians only because it stifles the potential of their faith in the constant creation of new life.

Chapter 4

Growth Through Honest Relationship

Parallels can be drawn between the relationship Becky had with me and the relationship Simon Peter had with Christ. Again, this is in no way presumptuous. My purpose is to demonstrate that the way people undergo fundamental change is an understandable process involving immutable natural law. I am not suggesting that Becky and I were similar to Peter and Christ. I am suggesting that insofar as Peter's response to his relationship with Christ was one of personal growth and development, it involved the same awesome natural forces that so frightened and changed Becky. Obviously, Christ's relationship with Peter involved a great deal more than personal growth, but I have chosen to address myself to this specific subject because it falls so legitimately within the scope of psychoanalytic investigation. Of course, the subject is also important because it is one of the central issues of the Christian faith and because the difficult times of the modern church are due largely to its inability to deal creatively with the subject.

Throughout the phase of development that we are now considering, Becky experienced me as a "great man."Her bigger-than-life view of me began with her discovery that my accepting attentiveness brought her a sense of comfort and relief which she had never had. This was more than a feeling of being cared for. She felt loved. She also felt she was participating in the analysis. To Becky, a person who grew up feeling that her very existence was a source of embarrassment to those who loved her most, the most gratifying aspect of her relationship with me was the feeling that in pleasing me she pleased someone more powerful than her guilt. At last she felt the peace and security she had searched for in illicit sex, drugs, and the pseudo-reunions she always had with her family after some particularly bad action.

Had the love Becky felt for me been based solely on my personal attributes, it would have been misplaced and shallow. It was, however, based on the healing nature of our relationship. Hence, her love was both gratifying and disturbing to her. Becky welcomed it and resisted it. And so it was with Peter's adoration of Christ. It was based on many things, not the least of which was Christ's personal characteristics (characteristics which have won the devotion of Christians for centuries). But as with Becky, Peter's relationship also contained an element of fear, if not terror. Obviously Peter loved Christ, but out of fear he held himself back from the full power of the relationship Christ offered. Even Christ's miracles, which appeared to rearrange the basic forces of nature, did not overcome Peter's reticence.

Miracles were a regular feature of life in the first century, and so one would not expect the followers of Christ to be swept into committed discipleship by a few wondrous acts. But the astounding catalogue of miracles which Christ had to perform before he received a single firm confession of faith from Peter, or from any other follower, compels one to conclude that Christ's followers were not just unimpressed; they positively resisted Christ. In the first seven chapters of Mark (Peter's confession of faith is in chapter 8), Christ cast out a convulsing, unclean spirit from a man in the synagogue at Capernaum, healed Simon's mother-in-law of a fever, ordered the paralyzed man who had been lowered into his presence through the roof to walk, restored a withered hand, stilled a storm at sea, cast demons out of a man so tormented that he broke the chains with which he had been bound, stopped the chronic hemorrhage of a woman who merely touched his garment, fed five thousand people with five loaves of bread and two fishes, walked on water, and restored the sight of a blind man at Bethsaida.

Quite obviously, the disciples' apparent inability to perceive and understand had little or nothing to do with the number or quality of Christ's miracles. It had to do with the meaning, the frightening messages of personal change, which the miracles imparted.

Miracles were (and still are) all that was needed to produce a transient audience of amazed followers. If Christ had wanted such an audience, he would certainly have yielded to one or more of the temptations presented to him during his period of retreat and decision in the desert. He chose instead to turn decisively away from an appealing Messiahship of social reform, surpassing miracles, or conquering military exploits. The disciples did not remain uncomprehending because they were dull men or because Christ's miracles were not sufficiently convincing. They held back because they intuitively realized that Christ was far more than his acts.

The scribes and Pharisees were much more openly

perceptive of Christ's real meaning than were the apostles. In the first twelve verses of the second chapter of Mark, for example, the scribes were deeply disturbed by the fact that Christ authoritatively forgave the sins of the paralytic who was lowered through the roof. Christ's preoccupation was with the man's sins, and this is what the scribes found blasphemous. When Christ followed through and cured the man of his paralysis, no one questioned and no one was upset. On the contrary, "they were all amazed and glorified God, saying, 'We never saw anything like this!'" The crowd received the amazement they wanted. The scribes were undoubtedly relieved because they knew they had him on legal grounds: one more miracle worker was no threat, but a man authoritatively interested in the heart and mind of humankind would have shaken the entire system by which they maintained their illusory equanimity.

The disciples could not so easily escape Christ's real meaning. They followed, and because they followed, they were there the next time Christ tried to get his message across. They were captivated by the man and so they could not escape, and because they could not leave they could not avoid either the disturbing message or the powerful relationship which were Christ's primary concerns.

As Becky tried to avoid the frightening but moving quality of our relationship by pleasing me with intellectual discussions of guilt, so Peter and the others tried to avoid the real impact of their relationship with Christ by following and imitating. Their yearning for help kept them trying for closeness, but their fear of the openness and scrutiny which a relationship with Christ entailed held them back. It is characteristic of frightened but needy people to attempt to get the help they desire by imitating an attribute of the helper. It is a way of feeling close to the source of help without experiencing the fear involved in examination and revelation. I am reminded of Joe, who had been spitting up blood for months. He was so terrified that he could not bring himself to have a chest X-ray, but he felt great relief from his anxiety when he arranged a weekly tennis match with a friend in robust health. The unconscious assumption was, "If I play tennis like my friend, I am healthy like my friend." Unhappily, he died.

In his miracles, Christ seemed to offer the disciples what they wanted; a close relationship with a powerful figure who towered above them, solved every problem, and saved them from the loneliness of decision and the fear of awareness. Indeed, when Christ spoke to crowds he often appeared willing to circumvent the facts of living. But when he spoke to those whom he called to become apostles, he resisted their efforts to achieve comfort under the aegis of his power. When the storm arose on the Sea of Galilee, Christ was not standing in the bow of the boat ready to take over as the disciples thought he should be. He was asleep. Because they wanted comfort, they assumed that if he did not spare them fear, he did not care. He did care—not for their comfort but for their growth, their rebirth.

New birth is not specifically mentioned in the first seven chapters of Mark, which we have taken as our reference point for this discussion. However, the conflict between the disciples' wish for a comfortable dependency on Christ the wonder worker, and Christ's insistence on a disturbing but growing relationship of searching openness with his disciples is always present. If there had been no conflict, the disciples would have had no reason to prolong their naïveté. Their apparent lack of comprehension was their way of following Christ and at the same time avoiding a confrontation with his real aim.

The scribes and Pharisees had everything to lose, and so they reacted openly and negatively to Christ. The disciples, however, thought they had found the security they wanted and so they did not react negatively, but neither did they react positively. When Christ finally forced a confrontation and asked Peter, "But who do you say that I am?" Peter appeared to give an affirmative answer: "You are the Christ" (Matthew 16:15 ff). But Christ was not convinced by Peter's declaration. Perhaps this is why he began to be explicit about the suffering he was soon to experience. Of course, this was a subject with which Peter should have been thoroughly familiar. He had witnessed countless conflicts between Christ and the powerful Pharisees. More importantly, had he been thoroughly involved with Christ he would have been familiar with conflict and suffering within himself. But Peter chided Christ for his teaching of suffering. He chided Christ because, in the hope of avoiding the suffering involved in facing his own hidden self, he had deliberately focused on Christ's awe-inspiring miracles. By emphasizing Christ's marvelous but not unique ability to perform miracles, Peter avoided a deepening awareness of his real self. At the point in time which we are discussing, Peter's following of Christ was largely a geographic phenomenon. By and large he was not yet a follower in the sense that he permitted his closeness to Christ to initiate within himself the fermenting process of discovery, acceptance, and decision which typified the life of Christ.

The prospect of a revealing relationship based on personal honesty was terrifying for Becky and it was terrifying for Peter. Eventually, Becky developed sufficient faith in the acceptance and understanding which characterized our relationship to reveal herself and find new birth. But when Peter declared, "You are the Christ," he was still a frightened man trying in his affirmation to avoid the searching, accepting, and changing relationship Christ demanded. In his affirmation of Christ, he denied that for which he yearned but feared to become: a child born anew.

Peter should have, and would have, known better if he had not clung to blinding simplicity. Had Peter looked, he would have had to see that Christ did not circumvent the suffering involved in his own personal searching any more than he interposed supernatural events between himself and the antagonists who constantly detracted from his message.

Peter was able to be a follower of Christ because he restricted himself from really understanding what Christ's fate was. Similarly, Nicodemus avoided Christ's pointed teaching on new birth by interpreting it with naïve literalness. In like manner, when the true nature of our relationship became obvious (that I was simply her doctor and not any of the things her fantasy offered), Becky tried to avoid personal tumult by superficially imitating me with intellectualized discussions of the psychology of guilt.

It is my belief that many modern Christians constantly do the same thing. They "profess" and they "follow," and in so doing they resist the personal struggle and change that is a central part of the Christian faith. Their apparent "love" of Christ is in fact a means by which they can maintain their personal equanimity. Their apparent devotion to Christ is a means of avoiding a sincere consideration of the facts of their own lives and the facts of life around them. In their distortion of the faith, they create the basis for most of the church's problems.

I am not suggesting that the obvious issues which confront the church are unimportant. I mean only to suggest that issues from sexual morality to racial integration to new liturgies are difficult for the average Christian to deal with because the average Christian firmly believes that his faith should spare him the pain of facing disquieting facts. Let me exemplify this in terms of the usual Christian response to youth and their problems with sexual morality. Aside from the wild behavior which characterizes the lives of a few youngsters, there are many sincere Christian young people who believe that it is unrealistic and even unhealthy to demand premarital chastity in our present society. They point out that responsible marriage at a reasonable age is impossible when social and economic independence cannot be achieved for the first twenty to thirty years of life.

There are many counter-arguments to be made to this idea, but, unhappily, the Christian community usually responds with a generalized declaration of Christian morality couched in highly selected words of Christ. Like Peter, today's Christian community prefers to profess Christ in a way which avoids the struggle that Christ went through. When faced with moral decisions, they prefer to quote commandments rather than to deal with the new facts and issues that must be considered if contemporary morality is to have a believable, workable basis. Of course, quoting the time-proven commandments appears to be a declaration of faith. It affords one a warm, noble feeling. In fact, however, such declarations avoid the anxiety of facing the uncomfortable feelings that would be aroused within oneself by an honest consideration of new facts and new moral arguments. But the honest young people whose lives are deeply affected by the church's stand on morality are not reached by such declarations. On the contrary, they call them fake.

Youth intuitively senses the worthlessness of postures which are pretenses of a closeness to Christ but which in fact isolate one from the wrestling that Christ endured as a part of his own development. Among Christian people, the gap between generations on moral concerns is not a mere matter of differing rules of behavior. The generations are divided because, while young people are forced to develop their morality in terms of their real desires, their Christian parents insist that morality is a simple matter of sustaining conclusions which they have never seriously questioned. The people of the church rarely answer the questions of their young people in a way which suggests that they know what it is like to grapple with temptation in today's world of indulgence. On the contrary, Christians answer the questions of their young people as if turmoil, temptation, and growth were limited to adolescence; as if maturity and faith relieved one of questioning. If Christian youth were to write a life of Christ based on the answers they get to their questions, they would tell the story of Christ's forty days of temptation as if it had been a six-week vacation at a desert spa.

I do not mean to suggest that Christians do not worry about their young people. On the contrary, they often agonize over them. Young people may appreciate the concern expended on their behalf, but they are at the same time estranged by it. The agonizing concern of Christian parents is all too often a circumvention of their own conflicts, and so it is no real basis for empathy or closeness with their troubled youngsters. Youth is not unappreciative. Youth has asked for help, but in the answers they get to their questions they see the underlying disbelief, the disengagement from the conflicts of growth that characterize the lives of their Christian parents. So they lose faith and then move on alone and unguided to repeat the pathetic mistakes of history. In the name of a "new morality" they encumber themselves with humanity's greatest and most hurtful restriction: personal chaos. Thus their potential for bright new life is lost to themselves and to the church. Of course, a few are hurt so badly that they run back to the church for the fixated security enjoyed by their parents. Tragically, these are the young people who represent the future of the Christian faith.

To carry my example yet further, let me speculate what the outcome of the conflict on moral issues might be if Christians felt that their faith demanded constant searching and new understanding. I believe that Christians of all generations would soon see that the enormous fuss that is made over the morality of sexual acts is largely a distraction from the real trouble. The real conflict is over the motivational basis for morality—whether one is moral out of fear and guilt or because morality ensures freedom and facilitates growth. To simplify this concept, let me compare it to the morality of obeying traffic regulations. The question is, does one stop at a red light because one is afraid of the police or because stopping facilitates getting to one's destination and also demonstrates genuine concern for the rights of others? Youth cannot and will not accept morality which is based on fear, maintained by guilt, and rewarded with a feeling of infantile specialness. They insist on and must have a morality which evolves from humanity's need to be free, to grow, and to care for others. To wish for freedom and growth is to love oneself. To care for the liberty of others is to love one's neighbor as oneself. The new basis for morality toward which many young people strive is far more consistent with Christ's summary of the law than the old basis to which so many adult Christians hold.

The problem I have exemplified in this discussion of youth and sex versus the typical response of Christian adults is repeated in every area of Christian life that requires an internal search. In some important instances, the church has begun to speak up on contemporary issues; but a follow-through that demands new insights and personal change will deeply disturb most Christians, because the Christian faith as they know it will be destroyed by personal, qualitative change.

Chapter 5

The Anatomy of Despair

The beauty of rebirth together with the satisfying sense of wholeness that always follows the experience brought Becky very close to me. Of course, she knew that it was her willingness to bear pain and her understanding that turned hatred of herself into loving acceptance of herself, but she also knew that she could not do it alone. She loved me with the tenderness and trust of a frightened child learning how to swim while buoyed up by her father's hand. Like a child, she could not progress simply because she was supported; she had to work. Neither could she learn while kicking and screaming in angry panic; there had to be a relationship.

Becky's life was changing so fundamentally that at times she could hardly recognize herself. When she compared me to the many well-meaning people who had tried and failed to help, it was quite natural for her to feel that I was "absolutely special." She assumed that my life with my wife, children, and friends was always loving and good. To Becky it could be no other way because, in her eyes, I understood everything; I had infinite patience; I always cared. She envied everyone who was close to me because she assumed that in such closeness they had found complete happiness.

Becky's relationship with me, however, was never quite what she wanted. She was never satisfied, as she imagined others to be, with me. There was always an element of fear and frustration in her relationship to me, but there were times of happiness and new freedom; joyous freedom that marked the end of a period of hating herself and the beginning of a period of new acceptance. Irrespective of her pain or joy, however, the natural forces of growth always pushed her at the same time to examine new, dark, and frightening corners of her mind. Each time that she conquered her fear and stepped forward into new areas of thought and feeling, she was a freer young woman.

Now, however, our relationship began to change. Becky became much less concerned with the freedom that she had begun to experience and more and more preoccupied with her desire for a closer relationship with me. Gradually she turned away from the searching curiosity about herself that had begun to open her mind. Instead, she became consumed with interest in my life. She spent her therapy hours asking me questions about myself. When I did not provide answers, she made them up and lost herself in daydream. Slowly and quietly Becky exchanged her growing freedom for the secure, tensionless bliss of fantasied closeness. The functional, real relationship between us that had developed out of her courage to search and my willingness to understand was displaced by endless dreams of contentment and satisfaction. The fear and anxiety, the pain and struggle of new birth were gone, but so also was the joy of new freedom.

Becky was occasionally able to see what she was doing. Once she described the current situation with a memory: "I was waiting for a bus after my hour yesterday, and I was staring at a tree. Suddenly my mind turned it into a beautiful Christmas tree, and then I remembered a very special Christmas morning when I was seven years old. My father came into my room and got me up before the rest of the family was awake. We went downstairs, and then he gave me the most wonderful bicycle I had ever seen. All he said was, 'You're a big girl now, I hope you'll enjoy it.' I don't think either of us ever understood why I dissolved in tears. I think I cried because the gift meant freedom, but all I felt was that I was losing him. It's the same with you. I don't want your freedom, I want you." Becky was in anguish. She knew that if she continued to work as she had, she would eventually have to give up her hope of extending the moments of safety and pleasure she had experienced with me. She said, "If I accept freedom, I'll begin to lose my hope of having a special relationship with you."

It was only the hope of ultimate gratification that had made the pain of openness bearable. And so Becky repeated the oldest paradox of human nature. She fought for freedom in the abstract because it gave her someone to follow and love, but she turned away from freedom that was real and personal because it was so lonely. All the insight that had been patiently garnered throughout our months of work, all the faith that had been built up out of Becky's courage to express the private truth, all logic and rationale was forgotten as she frantically sought to regain her original position of angry helplessness. Of course the more helpless Becky became in this new stage, the more omnipotent I looked to her. Once again she saw me as the great man who could save her life. Before she realized the consequences of freedom, she fought for it, but now she fought to regain the comfort of surrender.

Becky's fear of personal freedom may seem unusual, but it is not. It is, however, unusual for a person to see the issue of freedom so clearly that they are in a position knowingly to embrace it or to run from it. Becky turned away from the most important form of freedom there is— the freedom to think, to feel, to choose and to risk.

She turned back to the security of guilt and the comfort of adoration because she had reached a critical point in her work. She could not take one more step forward without realizing that she was no longer moving to please me but to fulfill her own deep desire to grow and change. Her memory of the Christmas bicycle was an accurate portrayal of the situation. Intuitively she knew that it would please her father to teach her to ride; it would bring them closer. But she also knew that he would soon expect her to respond to her own wish to go places on her own. She knew that once the training period was over, once she had mastered this new means of achieving a greater freedom, there would be a little less need in her life for her father's caring and watching. She intuitively knew at age seven that which she openly experienced in her analytic work with me.

And so Becky turned back to a relationship of inequality between us; a relationship in which there would be restrictions to rail against and also the hope of blissful security and total gratification. She began to search for freedom because she had found a relationship in which it was safe to express and accept all the things she had feared to face. She continued that process as long as it appeared that her search brought her closer to me and the gratification for which she yearned. She backed off from it when it became obvious that the growth she enjoyed destroyed the helplessness which fostered her hope that I would give her the anxiety-free existence of a loved child. In other words, Becky experienced with clarity that which most people perceive only dimly: that personal freedom is a joyous accomplishment that moves one toward constant renewal, but it also involves giving up the simple satisfactions that are due infants whose world is peopled by giants to be adored and placated.

Temporarily, Becky chose to adore me rather than grow toward an adult relationship, and I could not blame her because I came to realize that the most important and the most difficult thing she had to give up was the uncritical love she could feel for herself when she was absorbed with me. As it always is with youthful love, Becky felt wonderful about herself when she felt that I was wonderful. Young lovers have a peculiar awareness of themselves which permits a kind of self-acceptance that is not limited by the values which society, friends, and family inevitably place on various aspects of one's personality. To youth who have not yet accepted the limits and disappointments inherent in all relationships, love is an endearing reflection of themselves mirrored in the beloved. For the young, being deprived of someone to adore involves not only the loss of a loved one, but a loss of the means by which they enjoy uncritical love of themselves. A youngster who almost worships a star athlete is also proud of himself. He is sure that he can grow to be all the marvelous things he sees in his idol. But if he dares to take a closer look and observe the idol's shortcomings, he loses much more than an idol. He also loses some of the fantastic value he places on his own potential.

Becky preferred me to be an idol because it made her

feel good to be "the best patient of the best analyst in the world." This was very different from the loving acceptance of herself that she had accomplished through hours of digging out the hidden truth. She needed me then to help initiate and sustain the process of discovery, but she was always moving toward independence and freedom. Now she needed me because her love of herself was merely a reflection of her love for me. There was no freedom in her hero worship, but neither were there limits to her hope.

Becky tried in every possible way to sustain her fantastic convictions about me, but gradually the inexorable realities of life took over. When I was ill, she was deprived of her conviction that I could cure anything. When she overheard my angry telephone conversation with an auto mechanic, she had to realize that there were things I didn't handle with complete confidence. And then there was the bill; the monthly statement that, to Becky, always said the same thing—your doctor has to earn a living like everyone else.

Becky could not keep from turning back from her growing freedom, but she could not love herself for retreating. Now that the reality of my inadequacies bore in on her, she was utterly bereft. Becky had known disappointment and rejection; she had known fear and guilt; now she knew despair. She could no longer hope for fulfillment from me, because, relative to her wishes, I had insurmountable limitations. She could no longer love herself just because she loved me. I had failed her and so she hated me, and in turn she hated herself. As she once loved herself for loving me, she now hated herself for hating me. I was still a mirror but a broken one. She was disillusioned not only with me but also with herself. Her despair arose from the fact that in her bitter disappointment with me, she could no longer see herself as a beautiful person whose love and good intentions commanded my total attention. She despaired when she hated me, because she thought that her illusory goodness had captured me. She tried in vain to reconstruct her God-like picture of me and her beautiful picture of herself. She failed. She covered her face and wept. Session after session she wished she could die.

From time to time Becky had accused me of withholding things from her. I had. I always withheld knowledge which she absolutely had to gain from her own experience. For example, I could have told her that she was making me into an all-satisfying giant of a man who simply didn't exist. I could have told her that she did this because she didn't want to give up her hope of having her world made comfortably satisfying and because she so dearly loved feeling that she was the chosen favorite of the great man she insisted on making me. Occasionally I did mention these things, but I did not emphasize them because I really did not want to keep Becky from the process which eventually brought her to despair. I did not want her to avoid the bleak hopelessness which reality eventually brought her to, because despair is an essential part of growth.

Of course no one wants to believe that growing necessarily involves periods of genuine despair. Quite naturally one prefers to think that despair is avoidable. Becky was not unusual in this regard. But despair is in fact a natural aspect of growing, and people who grow throughout life have frequent periods of despair. People who manage to avoid despair also avoid growth.

In complete contradiction to the life of Christ and the lives of the apostles (we will consider the despair of Peter in the next chapter), the Christian church has almost made sustained, artificial hope an article of faith. As a result, Christian people have invented some very special ways of avoiding natural periods of despair, ways which have been perfected and codified over the centuries. One favorite, time-honored, and utterly workable method of avoiding the inevitable natural despair of growth is to replace it with unnatural gloom and suffering. The efficacy of artificial melancholy as a means of avoiding the despair of growth cannot be denied. The method has unmistakable advantages. An obvious one arises from the fact that, on the surface, the melancholy Christian appears to take all things seriously and to feel all things deeply. It is, therefore, quite natural for talented sufferers to rise to prominence in church affairs. (Chronic hemorrhoids are an enormous asset, too, since they give one a persistent appearance of pained attentiveness.)

In fact, sorrowful Christians do not take serious things seriously. They take seriously only their childish hopes for rewards and satisfactions. Behind their mask of pained patience lies the private hope of heroic justification. Troubles are a means by which the chronically afflicted can enjoy the fantasy that, because they are unappreciated by others, they are especially loved by Christ. Their bumbling treatment of the problems and troubles of their own lives and the lives of others arises from the fact that they do not see problems as matters to be worked out.

False sufferers appear to feel things deeply. Occasionally they do, but unfortunately for those who wish to share

Christian companionship with them, they feel the same emotion with the same depth in response to every situation. To such persons, pain is a stabilizing common denominator in all things. Holy Communion and a family picnic are essentially the same thing: trouble. Because they find the same problems in everything they do, nothing takes them by surprise and so they are never disturbed. They appear to be predictably stable but are in fact so involved in preserving their private hopes that they are simply unresponsive to the real world.

The real advantage in using false sadness to avoid the despair that naturally attends growth is that one is never out of control, never the victim of circumstances beyond one's personal control. Because Becky honestly hoped for gratification that was not available, she was frustrated and disillusioned. She could not help it. Ostentatiously sorrowing Christians, however, never experience pain as a consequence of frustrated hope. Their pain is a fulfillment of hope, because what they really hope for are petty frustrations which quash genuine hopefulness before it meets with the restrictions of reality. They never know the torment of having given everything to gain everything. On the contrary, men and women who use induced suffering to avoid natural despair always appear to have known right along that Christians who have dared hope for too much will only reap despair. In their righteousness, they justify their unmoving faith.

Some Christians, however, are simply not gifted in matters of obvious suffering. If they are to avoid the reality of periodic hopelessness, if they are to keep the faith, other means must be employed. One of the best is compulsive work: hard, driven, ceaseless work. Of course, work can be and often is a simple necessity of life. It can also be an ethical and loving response to the needs of others. When work is any of these things, there is a flexible, relaxed quality about it, and it is productive. Compulsive work is something entirely different. Compulsive work is a means by which the frightening, empty places in one's daily life are filled with external preoccupations. Ceaselessly busy Christians always offer a variety of "good" reasons for their work, but they usually avoid thinking through their real reasons for working. They assume, instead, that the essential goodness of the causes and projects to which they are devoted transcends personal questions. And that is exactly what driven work is supposed to do. It is supposed to draw one away from personal questions. It is supposed to pre-empt the time in which one might otherwise be alone to wonder what life is all about. Compulsive work is moral humanity's "speed." It is a drug which keeps life moving so fast that one is never caught in the natural processes of life, never subject to the cycles of hope and failure, joy and despair which move others toward greater development.

As with incessant melancholy, ceaseless work is usually accepted as a Christian virtue. But consider the effects of such work. Sometimes things are accomplished, but what about the people involved? Becky was never helped by her parents' "hard work." On the contrary, she saw it as "fake" and felt separated from them because of it. Of course, it was easy for her parents to account for the separation in terms of Becky's "laziness." But I suggest that Becky was put off because she sensed in the driven quality of her parents' work an underlying desire to escape from their own problems. In a sense they really were fake, but they could never be faulted for it. After all, they were good, hard-working Christian people.

The point is not to depreciate the virtue of hard work. The point is that insofar as compulsive work is used as a means by which one avoids the ups and downs of life, then one not only avoids the pain and the joy of one's deeper life, but also avoids genuine companionship.

Some people can invent absorbing concerns and compelling obligations with sophisticated genius. Driven by their fear of loneliness and despair, they create demanding parents out of schedules and conferences, manuscripts and programs, chores and duties. Like Becky, compulsive workers fear the disillusionment inherent in growing. Becky tried to circumvent her fear by making me into a giant who would make her life right and good. Compulsive workers make their projects and causes into giants who loom larger than themselves. Ironically, it is precisely the compulsively driven, over-involved man or woman—the person who appears to be the epitome of independent maturity—who at heart expects bliss, nurturing, and special comfort in return for his surpassing efforts.

Compulsive, over-dedicated work is not a Christian virtue in any sense of the word when one examines the true motivations behind it. However auspiciously and enthusiastically such persons begin their projects and involvements, however dedicated to the welfare of others they may seem, the result of their efforts is most often broken relationships. This happens because they do not work with a comprehension of what their work means to other people. Their primary concern is to fill up the gaps in their own lives. It is not loving. It is selfish.

Finally, compulsive work is not a virtue because it is a means by which men and women avoid growth and the despair that it involves. It is a sophisticated means by which one clings to the hopes and objectives of childhood. It is a means by which the vital growth process of life is avoided. Growth that is real is not a mere matter of hard work; it is a matter of responding to the disquieting facts of life. In fact, life that is growing regularly includes the death of hopes that are outgrown.

A third method that Christians use to avoid the painful, natural consequences of growing is divisive sectarianism. So much has been written on the social, economic, and theological causes and consequences of division within the Christian church, that I hesitate to spend even a few pages describing the process in terms of its use as a means of escaping despair and disillusionment. The process of breaking into smaller and smaller groups from a parent organizarion which has become less and less able to satisfy the demands of all the divergent groups which it subsumes is not limited to Christian groups or the Christian church. For that matter, neither are chronic melancholy and compulsive work. But divisiveness so glaringly contradicts the universalism for which Christ and the apostles lived and died, that one is safe in assuming that Christians are driven to divide within themselves by much more than ordinary social and group psychological pressures. That the Christian gospel is to be for all believers and is to bring all believers together is absolutely obvious throughout the New Testament. It is a major theme throughout the gospels from the nativity to the crucifixion of Christ. It is an important theme throughout the works of Paul from his argument with Peter over the circumcision party's exclusion of the uncircumcised to his death in Rome. Why, then, do Christians go on excluding each other? Why do they continue to pile up rationalizations and justifications for dividing themselves into smaller and smaller, more and more homogeneous groups?

There are several good answers, but the one I want to emphasize was clearly described to me by a teenager who was serving as a counselor at a neighborhood summer program for city children. The psychoanalysts who worked with the counselors were white. The counselors were black and the program was sponsored jointly by the local Episcopal and Presbyterian churches. All things considered, it was a fine mix. The group with which I was meeting was struggling with the problem of working with chronic troublemakers. Useful suggestions were made, but when the group moved on to discussing three or four youngsters who seemed impossible to reach, no one knew what to do. Then Bob, the teenage counselor I have mentioned, came up with an idea that met with immediate approval from ninety percent of his fellow counselors. "Kick them out and let them form their own group." Bob's solution was backed by facts and sound reasoning. He knew personally at least a dozen youngsters who had left the program because so much time had to be spent keeping order. Bob reasoned that it wasn't fair to deprive a dozen children in order to keep working with a few troublemakers who didn't seem to get anything out of the program. A few senior staff members added to the rationale for dismissing the "tough kids" by reminding us that the program was supported by contributions from people who wanted to feel that they were helping give a lot of deprived youngsters a good time. The staff worried about continued support if word got around that so many of them had left because they felt they could find more fun on the streets. Everyone pointed out that one capable senior staff person had quit the program because he came to "teach, not fight."

The logic and facts which supported dismissal were incontrovertible so long as we focused on facts of other people's existence—facts that applied to the children who caused trouble, the children who left, the feelings of the supporters, and so on. It was all strikingly reminiscent of the rationale Christians usually use to justify an act of exclusion. For example, when the minister of a large city congregation was asked why he supported a plan to move his church to the suburbs, he replied, "It is not fair for us to remain geographically distant from our people." And with that apparently forthright statement, no one thought to ask, "Who are your people?" or, "Yes, I understand, but what do you personally feel about the move?" Examples of exclusion are as numerous as factions. When liberal and conservative elements in churches try to exclude each other, they usually do it in terms of "what God wants."

But when I asked Bob why he personally wanted to kick out the troublemakers, the whole idea of exclusion took on a different light. His answer was, "Well, man, you see it's like this, I'm a little something like those cats myself, and I'd . . . what I'd really like to do is hit them right back. But then I'd be doing the same thing they do and I don't think, well, you see, I had my heart set on being junior counselor of the year and I know I'll never get it if I go around hitting people. I couldn't stand that, not just not getting to be junior counselor of the year but having to act like all those dumb kids." In other words, Bob's complaint was not with the kids themselves. He just couldn't stand them because they brought out an aspect of his own personality which he felt would put an end to his fond hopes of finding special favor in the eyes of the program administrator. So he wanted to get rid of the tough kids.

Fortunately, we didn't discharge the troublemakers and Bob was still chosen junior leader of the year (he also hit a few kids). As a result, the program grew, but more importantly, the people like Bob, who thought they couldn't stand to see their shining image of themselves tarnished, found that they could stand it, and they also grew. Because they kept the provocative children in the program, the junior leaders and staff alike went through some discouraging times. The junior leaders were always "upfront" about their discouragement. They said things like, "I just can't stand that little bastard; he makes me mad and then I feel bad about myself." After a clarifying statement like that, everyone would laugh in relief and find themselves closer to each other. They were relieved because someone had said what they all felt and, hence, they were closer to each other and better able to deal with their charges.

But the fine Christian leader who quit had said until the day he left us, "I feel so bad because I just can't get through to these children. I want so much to help. I can't stand the discouragement." Perhaps that is why he quit, but I suspect he quit for the same reason most of us quit things. (Quitting, particularly if you take a few people with you, is the same as excluding.) They quit because to stay with a group or program that includes stimulating, provocative people with differing ideas and feelings is to run the risk of not always being able to look like a "Christian," that is, a person who by carefully controlling the circumstances of his life manages to keep the vexing part of his own personality undisclosed. Such people never feel despair because they never see the evil in themselves, and thus they keep alive the illusion that their God-pleasing "goodness" will bring fulfilling rewards. Perhaps it does. But it does not bring growth. Growth is a process that includes periods of despair and genuine godforsaken hopelessness resulting from a fuller knowledge of oneself.

Chapter 6

Regression Forward

Becky avoided the personal impact of the truth which emerged out of our relationship by making me into a hero. In so doing she could listen to whatever I had to say as if it were a general axiom of life. Simon Peter did the same thing when he declared, "Thou art the Christ." In so doing he appeared to be devoted to the Christ while in fact he avoided the personal impact of Christ's truth. But Christ's talk of suffering-to-come exposed Peter's wish to have him on a pedestal. For this reason, Christ's response to Peter was swift and stern: "Get behind me, Satan! For you are not on the side of God, but of men" (Mark 8:32-33). The rebuke is so stern that it is safe to assume that Christ saw Peter's insistence that the Son of Man be above the pain and conflict of mortals as a virulent threat to his mission. Peter must have been shaken to the core of his being, but there is little evidence that he comprehended, let alone accepted, Christ's meaning. To Peter, Christ appeared to promise complete satisfaction and gratification above and beyond conflict and doubt. He was not about to be disillusioned.

Certainly Peter had grown to some degree. The very fact that he spoke up to Christ was a long and important step beyond the suppliant dependency he displayed in their first encounter. But irrespective of whatever change had occurred in Peter via the searching relationship Christ tried to establish, he was still unable and unwilling to relinquish his hope of having Christ on his own terms. I do not mean to suggest that Peter was unusually selfish. I mean only to suggest that human beings do not grow and mature without conflict and pain, and for most people growth involves a great deal of both. It is human nature now, and it was human nature in the first century, to back away from growth when it involves discomfort. It was and is natural for frightened, hurt men and women to choose dependency over independence and naïveté over insight. Persons who have experienced the fear involved in growing and are in retreat from it want a master, not a teacher of new ideas; a supplier of needs, not a guide to new life; a comforter, not a stimulator of personal change.

However shaken Peter may have been by Christ's rebuke, he did not have long to wait before he was once again comfortably ensconced in wishful thinking. Together with James and John, he accompanied Christ to the mountaintop and there he witnessed the transfiguration of Christ (Mark 9:2-8). The historical and theological significance of the transfiguration are matters beyond the scope of this book, but Peter's response to the event bears directly on the subject of growth. Peter wanted to build booths on the mountaintop for Christ, Moses, and Elijah. Peter wanted to erect a permanent marker. He wanted to hold onto the event. He was an awestruck child, not a participant.

Of course, Christ went right on talking about the inevitable earthly consequences of his disturbing work. In Mark 9:30-32, Christ once again talked of being delivered over to men who would kill him. And in the thirty-second verse, we are told that the disciples did not understand him and were afraid to ask him what he meant. Since

Christ was always eager to teach and explain his message, we can assume that the disciples' fear had nothing to do with Christ. They did not ask Christ for an explanation because they were afraid he might make his message so clear that they would have to understand him.

Again, this is like Becky. Becky knew that I was not the man she imagined I was. In her healthy mind she knew that I was not going to supply her needs or gratify her wishes. She also knew that because our relationship was a professional one, its duration would be limited. But Becky had tasted the freedom of growth and she was frightened of it. She knew it involved separation, loneliness, and risk. In other words, she knew that she was going to be bitterly disappointed in the situation, and she could not stand it. She did not want to hear me when I pointed out these facts. She did not want to understand. In like manner, Peter did not want to know what Christ meant. He did not want to face loss and separation but, more importantly, he did not want to face his own reactions to the loss of Christ. As we said with Becky, one who magnifies the object of love to unreal proportions also magnifies his or her image of self. Disillusionment brings much more than loss of the loved one. It brings loss of the boundless love of, and hopes for, oneself.

Peter wanted to escape the insights, the eye-opening consequences, of a relationship with Christ. He wanted to follow along like an enthralled pupil so concentrated on his teacher's abilities that he need never ask, "What am I learning?" Peter adored his teacher. Quite obviously he had become a devoted follower. He had learned, but had he changed?

When Christ sent the rich man away sorrowful (Mark

10:17-31), the apostles were astonished because riches were usually considered an indication of God's favor. The apostles could not understand Christ's demand that the man sell his possessions. If rich men, men favored by God, could not be saved, they assumed there was no hope for them. So Peter quickly reminded Christ that they had given up all to follow him. Christ responded with some reassurance that sacrifices would be made up. And then he added, "But many that are first will be last, and the last first." I suggest that this last statement was, in part, meant for Peter. Christ knew that the real giving up lay ahead. He knew that Peter hadn't really given up anything except the simplest of occupations to which he could return at any time.

Imagine the position of Christ at this point. He was just another wonder worker to the fickle crowds. He was hated by those in power and he was loved by a few men who would have fled in panic if they had dared understand what he was saying. Besides this, Christ's position was growing more and more urgent because he knew it was time to move on toward Jerusalem. He certainly knew that a confrontation with the authorities at Jerusalem had to end in his own death and the severest kind of test of his followers. He desperately needed committed followers who were aware of the consequences of their commitment and resolved to carry on their work. Instead, he was surrounded by men who confused devotion with infatuation, sacrifice with submissiveness.

The apostles had tasted freedom. Under the aegis of Christ's love they had superseded the Old Law. Or had they? Was the love that made the Old Law obsolete really theirs, or did they merely reflect the love of their leader?

Were they strong or were they simply able to act strong in the presence of their master? Did they believe what Christ said because they had experienced it, or did they simply love the man and accept what he said without understanding? Undoubtedly they had grown toward independence and freedom. Undoubtedly under the protective guidance of Christ they had faced many things about themselves and were therefore freer men. But as the crises of Jerusalem arose, as Christ's predictions of suffering, death, and separation became clearer, they gave up their brave new positions of personal development and regressed.

Peter was not alone in this. In Mark 10:35-38, James and John exemplify the situation I am describing. They ask Christ for the privilege of sitting at his right and left hand in glory. James and John are not newcomers to the group. They had heard what Christ had to say. They had felt the Man's revealing power and had sensed the demands it made upon them. Perhaps they were unsophisticated or even ignorant in spiritual matters when Christ began his work, but after they had heard him and lived with him for the better part of a year (or perhaps three years, if we accept John's account), they could not possibly make their childish request to sit at his right and left in heaven without purposefully turning away from the real impact and meaning of his message. When one considers that their request directly followed Christ's most recent attempt to explain the tragedy that was about to happen to him, one must recognize that their request was obviously a denial of glaring and terrifying facts.

Christ answered them by stating the obvious: "You do not know what you are asking." And when Christ spelled out the situation with, "Are you able to drink the cup I drink, or to be baptized with the baptism with which I am baptized?" James and John said simply, "We are able." Their answer showed no reflection or comprehension of the actual circumstances they were in. The other apostles were indignant with them, not because they themselves had openly faced facts and thereby understood the pathetic foolishness of the request, but because James and John had pre-empted them. They all wanted to be first. They were still children at heart; and the closer they got to the crisis which they privately suspected awaited them in Jerusalem, the more regressed and childish they became.

We arrive now at perhaps the saddest episode in the life of Christ. At the Last Supper (Mark 14:17-25), Christ made it clear that he would be betrayed by one of the Twelve. He had talked of his own impending suffering and death and had received little or no understanding from the disciples, but when they were told that one of them would fall from favor, they paid attention. Then, at long last, they were sorrowful, but probably not so much because they comprehended the inevitability of the death of their Lord. They were not sorrowful because they consciously realized that they had to lose him. They certainly were not sorrowful because they understood that the death of Christ was the plainest of all examples of humankind's murder of truth. The disciples did not reflect on the fear-based rage of the high priests and they said nothing to suggest that they understood from their own personal experience the violently disturbing quality of Christ's presence and message. They showed no understanding of the actual situation. They only asked, "Is it I?" (Mark 14:19). "Am I the one in trouble?"

It is essential that the reader realize that I do not

denigrate the disciples for their lack of comprehension and their selfish preoccupations. To do so would be to miss the entire point. The disciples were not "bad"; they were scared. They had become involved with Christ because he seemed to understand and care and because he did wonderful things. As time went on, they found that they were opening up within themselves. It was exciting, totally new and different, but they grew in order to please Christ, not because the truth Christ exemplified fermented within them. The change they experienced was an exciting adventure, not an inevitable result of having faced new facts. And then Christ began to fail them. He talked about dying at the hands of evil men and suddenly it was no longer exciting to change. Suddenly it was a deadly serious business, not just because Christ was going to die, but because his coming death forced them to realize that they were involved in a process that required them to die a little within themselves.

With Christ's announcement of his impending death, the disciples' faith was endangered. They could no longer grow to please a powerful parent. They could no longer grow because it made them feel good about themselves. Now growth had other consequences. New understanding was no longer a way to please the Master. It was an introduction to conflict—conflict which had to end in loss. Therefore, the impending loss of Christ was a tumultuous event, not just because the disciples loved him, but because without Christ to lead them, they could no longer accept the truth he preached simply to please him. With the death of Christ, his truth became a driving force that moved the disciples toward new awareness, conflict, acceptance and loss.

Awareness of new facts via Christ's teaching and presence always brought conflict. The disciples could not maintain their simple picture of themselves once they had met Christ. The new things they learned about themselves brought them into personal conflict, but out of conflict they found new acceptance. Then they grew and found new life, but still they did not realize that new birth was a new beginning—the beginning of loss. They were like Becky with her new bicycle. She loved it because it brought her close to her father, and she hated it because she knew it would take her away from him. As Becky backed away from the new freedom she had found, so the disciples, when they realized the consequences of their new freedom, turned away from it and sought safety in regression.

Christ's last encounter with Peter before the crucifixion took place on the Mount of Olives and in Gethsemane (Mark 14:26-42). It would seem that the disciples' behavior at the Last Supper had thoroughly convinced Christ that he was going to be deserted. Hence his statement: "You will all fall away; for it is written, 'I will strike the shepherd, and the sheep will be scattered.'" But Peter, still full of courage born of oblivion, announced, "Even though they all fall away, I will not." And Jesus said to him, "Truly, I say to you, this very night, before the cock crows twice, you will deny me three times." But Peter said, "If I must die with you, I will not deny you." And they all said the same (Mark 14:29-31). Having filled the night air with courageous words, Peter and the others lay down and fell sound asleep. They slept like children while their Lord awaited false arrest and murder.

When Christ first met Peter, he told him to let down his nets, but Peter protested because he had fished all night and had caught nothing. Peter could stay awake all night for fish, but he couldn't stay awake a few hours to pray with the man who had changed his life. Why? Because fishing did not scare Peter, but the thought of death because he embraced controversial, revolutionary truth terrified him. Peter and the disciples were not insensitive. They were terrified; they took the oldest and surest way out of such a dilemma—regression. They said fine things and then went to sleep as if words were enough. Indeed, from the frame of reference which they had adopted, words were enough.

Perhaps the reader who is used to thinking of the disciples' behavior as a prime example of humanity's ingratitude for God's gift of salvation will have trouble understanding my suggestions that the disciples were not ungrateful but were regressed. Perhaps readers will be helped if they recall the last time they visited a seriously ill patient in the hospital. There is a very good chance that the patient did not talk about the real problem—the possibility of dying. The patient probably slept most of the time and if he or she talked at all, it was to utter childish complaints about the food, the TV, wrinkles in the sheet, too much sunlight or not enough TLC. Such a person has handled terror by regressing. He or she has recaptured the perspective of a child, from which life's simplest aspects are all that matter. Like a child, the patient's world has no problem that cannot be solved by an adult. To children, there is no death; there is only sleep. There is no irreparable tragedy; there is only temporary loss of favor.

When Peter fulfilled Christ's prophecy and denied him, he wept. Christ had failed Peter when he did not overcome his adversaries, and if Christ would not be an all-powerful Father who handled everything, then Peter could not be a safe and secure child. In other words, if Christ was not just talking but really could be arrested, then Peter had to do more than just talk. Now there were real and dangerous consequences to the life he had been leading, to the ideas he had espoused. Christ failed Peter because he was real and not simply what Peter chose to imagine him to be.

Peter was human, and humans who are overwhelmingly disillusioned and frightened feel hate. Peter hated Christ for failing him and letting him feel fear, and that is why he wept in despair. He despaired because he had never really understood. Like a child, like Becky, Peter thought he was cared for because he was a good boy, a brave follower. Peter wanted to be brave and good, but Christ kept moving closer and closer to Jerusalem where the consequences of following were to become finalized. To contain his fear, Peter simply pretended everything would be all right and tried harder to please the man who would make it so. And then Christ was arrested and Peter's fear was greater than either his goodness or his bravery. At last his innocence, his naïveté, his goodness, and his brave words were not enough. Jerusalem showed Peter what he really was. He was shown up, and because he was human, I can assure the reader, he hated it. In his hatred, he assumed he could never be loved again, and that is the anatomy of despair.

Peter wasn't unworthy of love. If he had not been too frightened to comprehend Christ, he would have known that in Christ's scheme no one is worthy or unworthy of love; love isn't given according to worth. Over and over

Christ tried to make it clear that the love of God transcends worth. The prodigal was loved as much as his older brother. Peter's cowardice, like the prodigal's debauchery, was not his sin. His sin was his childish assumption that he had been loved for his "goodness." This is sin in the most important sense of the word because it is this assumption which causes people to drive a wedge into their minds in the hope of walling off the "bad self." It never works, and when the "bad self" comes out, despair is inevitable.

I do not mean to suggest that by understanding this cycle of events one can avoid it. To despair of being loved following failure to be righteous is human; it is a recurrent part of growth and must not be avoided. Peter could have avoided despair only if Christ had avoided Jerusalem and the cross. But then Peter would have died a fisherman and Christ, a forgotten prophet. On the cross, Christ despaired and felt forsaken. In the high priest's courtyard Peter despaired and wept. But these men changed the heart of humankind. And they changed the world.

Perhaps modern Christians too must give up hope and know despair—despair that deprives us of illusions and in the context of failure shows us more of what needs to be seen if we are to grow.

Chapter 7

Freedom Without Loneliness

Becky's painful despair continued without change for weeks. Then she alternated between brief periods of relief when she once again felt she was a favorite and long periods of renewed sorrow when reality again bore in. Her periods of relief were usually precipitated by a pathetic misinterpretation of mere coincidence. One day, for example, she arrived for her hour full of excitement and warm enthusiasm because a man who fitted my description had waved to her as she passed by the office earlier in the day. She believed completely that it was I who had waved. She even conjectured that since I knew what time she drove past the building on her way to work, I had interrupted my hour with another patient in order to be visible to her and to wave. While the illusion lasted, she was convinced that all of her despair and disappointment was simply part of a test through which I was putting her. She laughed with relief as she rationalized away all doubt, fear, sorrow, and anger. For a few precious moments Becky believed again that just because she loved and trusted me, I was hers and she was mine.

On another occasion, she chanced to read a short scientific paper on the subject of guilt which I had published. Again all her hopes were revived as she convinced herself that the entire article was about her. She was sure that her work with me had not only inspired the paper but had given me the insights and conclusions which it presented. Again she felt loved, and in turn she loved herself. Her hate and fear faded as she delighted in the belief that I had not failed her after all.

These and many similar events were important to her only because they dispelled her despair. The actual details of the events were quite unimportant. As a matter of fact, sometimes when she tried to recall what had made her so happy, she would confuse two or three such occurrences. Sometimes she would mix up facts which only a few hours earlier had catapulted her from despair to happiness. The facts were quite unimportant. The conclusion she reached was all that mattered.

Inevitably, however, reality and its attendant disillusionment re-emerged. To Becky each episode of despair seemed as bitter and hopeless as the first. But since I was in a relatively objective position, I could observe important changes in her thinking. Ever so gradually, Becky began to admit that she had to give up her fantasies and hopes of me, but not because I had failed her or because she had failed to live up to the standards which she imagined I demanded of her. This was a difficult thing to admit, because as long as either of us was to blame for the disillusionment she felt, she could go on hoping that perhaps some day she would meet someone who would not fail her and who would inspire pure goodness in her; someone who would be all hers. Becky began to realize that not possessing me and not being possessed by me was not a matter of failure; it was a matter of natural inevitability. Gradually she realized that she lost me in exactly the way an infant loses its mother's breast when it develops teeth. In other words, her insistence that one or the other or both of us had failed was a way of holding onto her child's hope. When at last she realized that her loss was not a failure and no one, therefore, could prevent it, the way was cleared for genuine mourning.

The grief of mourning is quite different from despair. There is always anger, failure, and bitterness in despair, but mourning is full of yearning and wishing, recounted memories and tears. Despairing people have no relief except as they delude themselves into thinking that everything is all right again; but mourning is a merciful process. The mourner cries over his or her loss, talks of memories, cries again, and then feels relief, in a recurring sequence. Depressed and despairing people never really give up the object of their hopes and wishes, but mourners, although it may take months, do. Mourning people feel that they will never be able to replace the lost loved one, but they do not feel unloved or unloving. And finally, despairing people tend to desire isolation. They want to be left alone in their suffering, but mourners desire company with whom they can share their grief and thereby eventually move on.

As Becky progressed from depressed, angry despair toward mourning, she once again began to share her feelings. Over and over again she recounted her experiences with me. She recalled each moment of insight, each step forward into freedom, the painful disillusionments and the understanding and independence which always followed. She was about to resign herself to sorrow when, with help, it occurred to her that her sorrow, perhaps even her despair, was a preparation for a new and greater step forward. As the notion germinated in her mind, she realized anew that the fulfillment of her childish wishes would have been antithetical to her growing desire for a fuller, more complete freedom. Becky's hopes and wishes, however, did not fade away with this renewed realization. She grieved as she recalled and re-experienced the ardent desire for comfort and security for which she had so often sought satisfaction.

Gradually, very gradually, she began to realize that the crucial deficit in her life was not a lack of love from her parents; it was the complete lack of a sense of growing, with its losses and gains, its fears and joys, that had kept her fixated on the desires of childhood. In Becky's life, every stage of development had been associated with trauma, which always made forward movement frightening. Relinquishing the security of old and familiar ways appeared to be a cruel trick. She recalled that when she was five years old she could hardly wait until she was six and able to start school. She wanted to grow, but then just before school started, her mother got a good job which necessitated her leaving Becky alone for several hours a day. Her mother expressed regret, but she excused her absence with the idea that since Becky had to go to school, she was free to work. Becky was terrified during the hours she spent alone in the house. She was angry at her mother for leaving, and frightened to express her anger for fear it would drive her mother further away. Now she hated school because it was no longer an exciting step forward. School meant the loss of mother, fearful loneliness, anger, and guilt.

With this kind of realization, something very new developed in Becky's analytic work. She began to forgive.

She began to see that, while there were special traumas in her life which occurred when she was too young to understand, no one's life is without serious trauma. Eventually Becky forgave me for the pain I had caused her, and then she discovered something that brought her the first touch of genuine joy she had ever known. As she understood, she forgave, and as she forgave, she awakened to a joyous sense of freedom without the fear of loss. She awoke to the fact that freedom born of one's understanding, acceptance, and forgiveness need not be lonely. On the contrary, it is the only lasting basis for companionship. She knew now that the only limit to her freedom was her own fear that in growth and change she would be alone. The freer she was willing to allow others to be to err in relationships, the freer she was able to be with herself. The more she was genuine about herself, the closer she felt to those she loved.

Now Becky wept again, but not in despair or sorrow. She wept in joy and satisfaction at finding that the natural thrust of her life toward greater development and less fear, more freedom and less guilt, did not lead to separation but to companionship. Her life moved toward a communion with growing men and women. The loss of childhood no longer meant abandonment to Becky. The anxiety of new challenge no longer meant there was something terribly wrong. She was free, joyously free. She had lost all hope of getting what she thought she wanted when her life was directed by fear and guilt, false hopes and anger; but she had found in abundance the only thing she wanted now that her life was growing. She loved and was loved in freedom.

Becky had not talked to other people about her

treatment for a long time, but now she wanted to express herself. When friends had worries and conflicts, she found herself listening rather than walking away. She found herself caring whether or not they were helped. She was willing to express ideas that she knew were helpful but which did not necessarily bring credit and recognition. She worried that her friends could not accept her the way she now was, but, to her surprise, the only friends she lost were those who had used her trouble as a means by which they could express their own self-righteousness—people who in their own way were unwilling to be free. There was pain in these losses, but they too occasioned a still greater discovery.

Prompted by several such losses, Becky experienced all over again her loss of me as an all-gratifying parent. In this final reworking, Becky discovered that in loss she had herself become the strong, understanding person she had always wanted for a parent. She had lost me, and in her loss she had become something of what I had been to her. Becky was transformed. Her joy was quieter, deeper, and more lasting. Once she had yearned to be cared for, but now in a mature and honest way she cared for others. She once demanded independence, but now she had freedom. She once hoped for closeness, but now she had companionship. She once yearned for love, and now she loved.

Becky's realization that her past was not so unusual is important for us to bear in mind as we seek to adapt her experiences to the lives of Christian people. Her early experiences were particularly hurtful only because they occurred before she had the mental tools with which to process them: language and the ability to conceptualize, and the capacity to maintain a relationship in spite of severe frustration. Because of the very early rejection she experienced, Becky felt everything acutely; she reacted to every problem dramatically. However, most of the trauma she met in life is common to most of us, and while her reactions were exaggerated, they were typical of troubled people who are without help.

Too many Christian people are tragically and unnecessarily without help in matters of personal psychological growth. The unhelped condition of Christians is tragic because, when left to themselves they, like Becky, pervert the best things in their lives. To avoid the stirring effects of love and affection, they turn to pain and guilt. To avoid the risks and uncertainty of freedom, they choose stifling security. And to avoid despair, sorrow, and growth toward joy, they cling to the tenuous delights of childhood. It might be protested that Christians are, after all, only human, and humans make grievous errors. But Christians are not only human. We are human beings with a faith that can encompass error while we are led toward growth.

Growth to many Christians is a mere matter of accretion, a gluing on of new insights that support the convictions with which they are already comfortable. But growing is not quantitative increase. It is qualitative change. Growth is not a matter of continual mental exercises which add to one's psychological stature. Growth involves continually living through the natural cycles of hoping, despairing, losing, and finding joy. In spite of the example of Christ, however, Christians fear growth. They fear it because it is beyond their control; it is a natural process. They hold back their bitterness and their angry despair because they are afraid. They hold back their love and their hopes. They never mourn loss because they have never known intimacy; therefore, they miss joy. The Christian church is sometimes a joyless marketplace for pleasantries when it was meant to be a living community of men and women who are free to express and exchange their most meaningful ideas and emotions. It was meant to be a place where love has made it safe to search out a new self as the hatred and pain of old mistakes are relinquished.

The church was meant to be a place where honest expression changes despair into the sorrow of loss and the joy of growth. But often Christians feel they must withhold themselves, their thoughts and feelings, until at last despair drives some of them out of the church. Once out, they may find some "New Age" philosophy in which to reveal themselves, or they may just grow old.

The revived effort to document the historical Jesus has offered Christian people a unique opportunity to re-examine their faith. Many Christians do not have a rationale which supports their faith in an age of scientific "certainty." With such a fragile foundation, Christians sustain their faith by not knowing what the rest of the world thinks. Most Christians are not therefore in a position to evaluate the new ideas which bombard us from all sides. Without a core rationale that supports growth and development, we are left with the comfort of childish concepts which precludes any integration of new information.

Christians dread disbelief. They seem to feel that they can grow and develop without searching out the inadequacies of their belief. No wonder they are often held in contempt by the scientific world. In response to new findings, scientists are constantly having to give up theories and ideas to which they have devoted their lives, and arrive at "We don't know. . ." In like manner, Christians since ancient times have grown by virtue of periods of disillusionment when everything they believed God to be seemed to be false. There is no major difference between the scientific tradition and the history of the living faith in this regard. The difference is between believers who are periodically disappointed, and unbelievers who are comfortably sure that God is dead or irrelevant. The difference is that growing believers are constantly wishing, hoping, suffering through disillusionment, and finding new growth and joy, while people, scientists or not, who are locked into "scientific dogma" hope for nothing beyond themselves and, therefore, are never disappointed, never growing, never truly joyous.

The now-deceased "God-is-dead" people used to assure us that they were already free of the uncertainties of faith. In my experience, however, what they really meant was that they were comfortably free of the disquieting hope of joy. Their philosophy moved nowhere, and so they assured the world that they had arrived. They affronted the church with bold talk, while in their stolid certainty they displayed the worst and most unchanging aspects of religion.

The joy of mature faith is a result of growing. It is a natural result of a natural process. Joy is not an achievement; it is a happening of development. It is the emotion of people who have discovered that in separation they have developed the strength and compassion they once loved in someone else. Joy cannot be analyzed by observers, but it is understood by those who have participated in the process of growing which precedes it. Mature joy, therefore, is a thorn in the flesh to those who gain childish security from their intellectual machinations. To such people anything which they cannot reduce to simplistic terms simply does not exist. They may even assure the world that they are scientific, but they are merely frightened of anything which surpasses their limited comprehension. And that is the antithesis of science.

Since joy is the natural outgrowth of the Christian gospel, one might expect Christians to embrace it. But often they do not, because they too are afraid. Indeed, joy is unnerving because it consummates growth. Because it is the natural result of a natural process, joy sweeps aside all of the resistances we have mentioned. Guilt, false melancholy, hard work, sectarianism, naïveté, regression, and intellectualism are all means by which we may impart an illusion of control over our lives—and control is basically inconsistent with joy.

This is why Christians are so much more comfortable with the joy of Easter than with the joy of Pentecost. Easter joy is experienced as a response to what happened to Christ, while Pentecost is a spontaneous expression of what continues to happen to his followers. Joy that is justified by the power and success of someone else requires no personal growth. By definition, joy that bursts forth as part of a natural process within oneself requires personal change.

However appropriate joy may seem in the Christian faith, it is often resisted—because it absolutely must be shared. Real joy, joy that consumes one, is never unrelated to others. On the contrary, joy compels one to speak out in the hope of involving others in the emotion. Joy is the emotion of men and women who have lost everything and have genuinely despaired of earning the special love they once craved. Such people have learned through sorrow and loss that there is no need to surpass their brothers and sisters or maneuver themselves into a more deserving position. In the defeat of private hopes built on individual worthiness they have found a basis for true community.

Joy is all too rare in the Christian community, which should be alive with it. It is rare because, given the usual teaching of the church, Christians seldom have to learn that which every analytic patient must experience a thousand times: hopes of fulfillment supported by appealing and suppliant goodness, melancholy, hard work, or right thinking may bring illusory comfort and moments of "blessed assurance," but not joy. For joy is the emotion of men and women who have seen the true nature of humanity in the assembled facts of their own lives; men and women who in loss and sorrow have become the giving persons whose bounty they once failed to earn. Joy is the emotion of transformation.

Chapter 8

Then Joy Breaks Through

The transformation of all time and the Christian proto-type of joy is the resurrection of Christ, its celebration the high point of the Christian year. However, despite all its momentous theological significance, the resurrection of Christ and its celebration seem to stimulate very little transformation and joy in modern Christians. This is not all that surprising. Christ's transformation from death to life and the promise of a similar change for all believers is a happy prospect which affords many people great comfort. But it is rarely a source of genuine joy to us, because it is about someone else. The resurrection, like the miracles of Christ's day, was awesome, but not joyful. Its chief product was confusion and, at least for Thomas, disbelief.

Overdressed Easter morning Christian congregations have no more success finding genuine joy in Easter than did the apostles. By and large, joy is a "now" emotion. It is an emotion associated with personal change in the present. Easter, as it is usually celebrated, is neither personal, present, nor transforming. On the contrary, it is celebrated as a memorial, a time of remembering what happened to someone else a very long time ago. What the celebration should help us with is reliving the resurrect-ing events of our own lives. Only in that understanding of transformation do we have any real hope for the ultimate resurrection.

Science puts a damper on the happy expectations which Easter arouses in most Christians when it clearly questions the physical resurrection as a "real" event. But happy hopes of total and everlasting fulfillment are hardly the essence of Easter. Science does not ruin Easter; it only challenges the meaning which Christians who have not experienced their own resurrecting events prefer it to have.

No event in the history of Christendom has suffered so much crippling distortion. I have no desire to question the faith of persons who are satisfied that Christ physically arose from the dead, unless that event acts as a means of keeping alive the hopes and wishes of immaturity and provides an escape from the natural foreclosure of childhood, which is an essential prerequisite to growth.

To most Christians, the theological significance of Easter has never been resurrected. It lies buried in a hallowed tomb of dreams. When belief in the resurrection acts in this way, the entire Christian faith becomes a gigantic resistance to growing up. Then the devastating criticisms of Sigmund Freud are true. I am not concerned that these remarks will harm anyone's active faith, because it is my experience that persons whose beliefs are the product of a continuing personal search are not perturbed by criticism. The dramatic and sometimes vituperative response which scientific criticism occasionally calls forth from the Christian community is always from persons who see in any such challenge a threat to their expectation of inheriting the earth simply because they are good children. The response of such people is a modern enactment of the attitude of the prodigal's older brother.

(Luckily, the faith teaches us that God is as forgiving as the father in that story!)

As a psychoanalyst I am aware that some people cannot feel that life is worth living unless they can hope for fulfillment of the unrelinquished desires of childhood. At one time or another, every analytic patient cries out in pain, "You are ruining my life, you are taking away everything I've hoped for," when in fact all the analysis has done is lay bare the impossible infantile desires that lie behind guilt, shame, endless restrictions, and burdensome righteousness. But the need of modern Christians to think through their faith and find in it a living source of constant renewal and growth is too great to be put off; despite the pain, the process must not be stopped.

Psychologically speaking, the post-resurrection appearances, which are cited as proofs of Christ's presence, changed nothing. It is precisely because the Easter event did not necessitate change on the part of the followers of Christ that Christians now celebrate the event so comfortably. But Easter is not a renewed promise that everything one has ever wanted is going to come to pass. However appealing such a prospect may be, honest men and women of our time just can't believe it. Consequently, their joy in Easter is painfully artificial. However important the physical resurrection was to the apostles, it is used by modern Christians as a decoy.

Psychologically, the overriding signficance of Easter is not the physical resurrection. Today, after two thousand years of learning about natural phenomena, belief or disbelief in the physical resurrection is a distraction from the unnerving fact that the truth personified in Christ lives, and cannot be destroyed by disbelief any more than it is created by belief. It is hard for most Christians to grasp the idea that the powerful resurrecting truth of Christ lives on whether or not they believe in the physical resurrection. Like Becky, who said, "I don't want your freedom. I want you," Christians do not want Christ's truth; they want him—to the exclusion of his truth.

Truth in the abstract is in fact of doubtful power to change anything. It must be personified. People do not change just because they face facts but because they love the person who represents the facts to them. In this regard Easter raises a truly momentous question: Who will personify the truth of Christ? The usual answer is: Christ will. Christians give their answer the ring of loyalty and of affirmation. In fact, it is simply an honest recognition that if Christ's truth is to be personified by anyone, it will have to be Christ himself. Most Christians sense no continuing change within themselves that makes them feel equal to the task of personifying Christ's truth. But there is only one answer that is both theologically sound and consistent with the need of modern people to grow. And that is, "I will personify the truth of Christ as I experience it in my own life."

This is the only answer to the question Easter poses. It is the only solution to the problem raised by the resurrection. But we resist it, because to become a personifier of Christ's truth, to give it life with one's own life, is to lose Christ as an indulgent parent and a fufiller of favorite fantasies. It is to hope and to lose hope, to despair and to mourn. It is to know the joy of change and sharing. It is to grow.

The defensively naïve can only boast unchanging belief in the resurrection as an indication of true faith, and in so doing they need never suffer through the development which the truth of Christ demanded of the apostles. The apostles believed in miracles; but unlike modern men and women who claim that belief, they were never spared the conflict which always accompanies truth that has been lived out in a life of courage and love.

One wishes that anyone who is in earnest about confirming the living presence of Christ in their lives today could do so by submitting themselves to the penetrating truth of his gospel as it is lived by the believing community. The hoping and disillusionment, bliss and mourning, loss and transformation which inevitably follow are verifications every bit as real as the experience of the apostles.

Any attempt to verify the basis of the faith can, however, lead to an endless detour. Bill, a former patient of mine, continued in treatment in spite of the fact that he never was able to be part of a helpful process. But he wouldn't leave, because he didn't want to be alone. Rather than stay or leave because of what I actually was to him, he chose to avoid both the pain of leaving and the reality of staying by hanging on because a friend had told him that I was a good therapist. I suggested we terminate the therapy. Such fence-straddling can defeat any attempt at verification of the faith.

The description of post-resurrection events on the basis of known natural phenomena which follows is not meant to replace belief in the events. For that, one would have to assume that today's science is at a satisfying end point in its search for understanding. It is not, and nothing is more unscientific than to assume that it is. Scientific explanations of supernatural phenomena can also be in error when one does not recognize the natural function that belief in the supernatural plays in normal human psychology. Without a normal belief in the supernatural, modern people are confined to the artless logic of their computers, and that is an important first step toward futile despair. Twentieth century people are not universally depressed because they have failed to reach the rational utopia toward which they have been striving since civilization began. They are depressed because they have realized that rationalism itself is unbearable and inhuman.

Christianity shorn of its miracles and its resurrection is not more scientific; it is simply less human. For example, a scientific explanation of the apostles' post-resurrection experiences is helpful only if it defines more clearly the natural processes involved without precluding the supernatural. Even the joy of growth and transformation is worthless if it can be achieved only via a rationalism that pre-empts our humanity.

If we remember how Becky interpreted reality in ways which gave her relief from despair, it becomes obvious that we need not question the sincerity of the apostles' accounts of the post-resurrection appearances. It has been said that either the resurrection occurred or the world has been the subject of a gigantic fraud. These are not, however, the only alternatives. Given the painful sense of despair which possessed the followers of Christ after the crucifixion, it would be quite natural for them to be open to interpretations of reality which would give them passing relief. When one remembers that this happens today to relatively healthy people who suffer despair in response to overwhelming loss, it is quite reasonable to hypothesize that such a thing could have happened even more convincingly to first-century men. I personally have no doubt that the apostles psychologically experienced the physical presence of Christ after the women found the tomb empty. Their reports are completely sincere. They are not deceptions; but by the same token, they do not convincingly suggest, let alone prove, the physical resurrection of Christ.

Consider the story of the appearance of Christ to the two followers on the road to Emmaus (Luke 24: 13-35). The two men were walking and talking about the momentous events of the day when Christ appeared and asked what they were talking about. Interestingly, the men did not recognize him, so they responded with, "Are you the only visitor to Jerusalem who does not know the things that have happened there in these days?" and he said to them, "What things?" The men went on to describe their loss of Christ (whom they had hoped would redeem Israel), the women's report of "a vision of angels, who said that he was alive," and the apostles' finding the tomb empty. Christ then admonished the men for not realizing that these things had to happen according to plan, but the men still thought they were talking to a badly informed stranger.

When evening came, the two men asked the stranger to stay with them. They sat down to eat, and, "When he was at table with them, he took the bread and blessed, and broke it, and gave it to them. And then their eyes were opened and they recognized him; and he vanished out of their sight." The two men did not consider the possibility that their friendly stranger was Christ until he performed a common and familiar act which both powerfully reminded them of their loss and could be interpreted in a way that would reverse their loss. The moment they interpreted the blessing and breaking of bread as a sure sign of the presence of Christ, they began to go over the things he said and reinterpret them in a way that confirmed their conclusion. In other words, there is a strong possibility that they did exactly what Becky did when she yearned for relief from her state of hopelessness. When Becky saw a man who fitted my description wave to her, she had in fact seen me. But I did not wave; I had simply gone to the window to water the begonia I keep on my windowsill. My waving was Becky's interpretation of a common act which she had seen me do dozens of times. The act both powerfully aroused her yearning and, if correctly misinterpreted, offered relief from her yearning. In relief, Becky went over the events of the recent past and reinterpreted them in such a way that she could believe that I was once again hers and she was mine.

Having made clear that the psychological interpretations which I offer are meant only to provide the modern believer an awareness of ideas which might revive the willingness to search, let me also suggest that the post-resurrection experiences were not a lasting source of joy. They could not be, because they only revived hope; they did not foster change. After these appearances the apostles were just as slow to catch on and just as unmotivated to do their work as ever. If anything, they were more child-like. Contrary to the common belief of Christians, the resurrection did not change the apostles; it simply gave them relief. They were still amazed children quite incapable of taking on the tasks which Christ had in mind for them. For example, Peter, according to the Gospel of John, had gone back to fishing. And once again Christ had to tell him where to let down his nets. Peter hadn't changed much.

The immaturity of the apostles after Easter is not just a matter of psychological conjecture. That they lacked an essential quality is clearly referred to by Christ in Luke 24:49: "And behold, I send the promise of my Father upon you; but stay in the city, until you are clothed with power from on high." Perhaps the clearest indication that Christ realized the need for further growth on the part of the apostles is in John 16:7: "Nevertheless I tell you the truth, it is to your advantage that I go away, for if I do not go away, the Counselor will not come to you; but if I go, I will send him to you." In John 16:12-13, Christ continues: "I have yet many things to say to you, but you cannot hear them now. When the Spirit of Truth comes, he will guide you in all truth." Clearly, Christ realized the fragile incompleteness of his apostles. It is just as clear that Christ knew that their growth toward becoming men of convincing power depended on their losing him. Only in loss could they gain that which would transform them.

In despair the apostles yearned for the presence of Christ, and they did in fact experience Christ's presence. I suggest that they did so for the same psychological reasons that Becky (in a less intense way) experienced me in various situations after she felt she had lost me. Interestingly, the apostles did not react to Christ's presence with joyful welcome. For example, Matthew 28: 17: "And when they saw him they worshipped him; but some doubted;"

and Luke 24:36-38: "As they were saying this, Jesus himself stood among them. But they were so startled and frightened, and supposed that they saw a spirit. And he said to them, 'Why are you troubled and why do questionings rise in your hearts?'"

Two things are clear. The appearances of Christ were not so convincingly real as to erase all doubt about his physical reality. Certainly the apostles did not hesitate because the appearance of Christ contradicted their scientific frame of reference. If that were the case, they could never have accepted the transfiguration, walking on water, or the raising of Lazarus. They hesitated because, having re-experienced the presence of Christ, the reality of what he was and what his life demanded of them again bore in on them. In a word, they were ambivalent. They yearned for him as they wanted him to be. When they saw him, they were reminded of what he actually was.

John, a young man of my acquaintance, was overwhelmed with homesickness as he awaited overseas embarkation in military service. Hearing of their son's trouble, his parents flew out to see him and comfort him. Although John knew his parents were coming, he seemed shocked when he saw them. The parents were almost in a state of shock themselves when, after only five minutes, their son began to provoke an argument with them. He actually questioned the sincerity of their visit. Obviously the soldier yearned to see his parents, but not as they actually were, only as he wanted them to be. He was shocked, and he argued to circumvent his disappointment in the reality. In his fear and loneliness, he yearned to see them, but when they appeared, he was confronted with the realization of who they really were, and that was quite different from what he wanted them to be.

The apostles believed in Christ's physical presence, but they still had to wrestle with the truth he represented. Since acceptance of the miracle of resurrection did not contradict the apostles' knowledge, they were not so preoccupied with the event that they forgot the man. However, for modern people to accept the resurrection in the same way the apostles did, they must blind themselves to facts which are common knowledge. The result is an anxiety-producing intellectual conflict. Modern Christians have confused the anxiety and disbelief they feel when they try to believe in the physical resurrection with the anxiety the apostles felt when they were confronted with Christ, the Man and his truth. The two things are simply not related. The crucial difference is this: conflict which arises out of the intellectual problems involved in a belief in the physical resurrection is (given modern knowledge) both endless and futile, while conflict which arises out of a confrontation with the personal meaning and purpose of Christ's presence is growth-producing. It is the difference between sterile intellectualization and an ongoing involvement in a process of growth which transcends one's own thinking and constantly moves one toward new life.

Christ was never willing to allow his followers to rest on their naïve amazement with his miracles. On the contrary, to Christ the real test of faith was a man's response to the truth he personified. Hence, the important issue for modern Christians is neither naïve belief nor unthinking disbelief in the physical resurrection. The issue is the same as it was for the apostles: involvement in or detachment from the fermenting growth process which the love of Christ, the Man and his truth, inevitably induces. The issue for modern believers is whether or not they will become so distracted by their belief or unbelief in the physical resurrection that they will miss the utterly essential truth of Easter—the truth that in response to hopeless loss we can gain new life, life transformed.

I have elaborated on the matter of the physical resurrection, not because it is still hotly debated among Christians, but because it is a prototype of Christian expectations and actions. The Christian view of Easter determines whether we accept the anxiety and disappointment of today's involvement as part of present growth or whether we avoid involvement and wait for changes to be imposed upon us in some painless way at some distant time.

By the time of Pentecost, Peter and the others were no longer experiencing the physical presence of Christ. They had been through periods of despair, renewed hope, loss, and mourning in relation to Christ. Now they were on their own . . . but were they? They chose Matthias to replace Judas, and then they gathered in the Upper Room. Christ had appeared in the midst of them before. Would it happen again? Undoubtedly they yearned for an appearance in the same way as a student who has finally begun to master a difficult problem on his own may yearn for a return of the old days when he was naïve and the teacher was magnificently beyond him. But the apostles had begun to do things on their own. They had begun to change.

My suggestion is that while sitting in the Upper Room (Acts 2), they were powerfully reminded of their Lord.

Undoubtedly they talked of their wish to have him with them again. They probably prayed as he had taught them, and assuredly they went over the experiences they had shared. Perhaps it was a hot day. Perhaps an afternoon breeze came up, a curtain moved, and the group was galvanized in expectation of another appearance of Christ. But it did not happen and renewed sorrow overcame the group. Then someone, perhaps Peter, looked across the table and began to realize that his sorrowing brother looked different to him. He looked different because through his suffering Peter now saw his brother with the same compassion, understanding, and love with which Christ had seen them all. Suddenly he sensed that in losing all hope of fulfillment for his cherished and immature desires to be the bravest and truest disciple, he had gained the capacity to love as Christ loved. Christ was no longer outside him, a comforting vision in times of sorrow. Now Christ was in his being. Now Peter and the others knew the consuming joy of transformation, and they spoke like men on fire, speaking unselfishly to all. Now the resurrection of Christ was validated, not by visions born of hope, but by personal change from sorrowing impotence to joyous forcefulness. The resurrection was confirmed in Peter by his change from bravado to honest daring. He had been erratic; now he was a man of persuasive conviction.

Relative to its personal importance, many Christians appear to ignore Pentecost. But they do more. They actively resist an appreciation of it by surrounding the event with caution and suspicion. The caution and suspicion appear to be a rational reaction to the over-emphasis which a small minority of Christians place on the experience of speaking in tongues. In the minds of most Christians, glossolalia has the aura of perversion. But to such people so does everything else that is joyous fun. Given appropriate circumstances (I myself prefer the shower stall), glossolalia is neither fearsome nor perverted. It is a pleasurable expression of feelings which are garbled by the use of syntactically correct language. I direct the attention of the skeptical to the original speakers in tongues—babies. Babies have feelings and they express them without words. It is not precise communication, but, as any well-bedded couple knows, words are not the only vehicle one can use for the expression of intimate, over-flowing joy. They may even hamper it.

So why do Christians shy away from Pentecost? Certainly not just because of tongue-speaking. That is as unimportant as the fact that the apostles met in an upper room. Christians are leery of Pentecost because it is a joyous celebration of personal transformation from fear and dependency to independence, freedom, and joy. Most Christians just don't want to face the fact that they haven't progressed that far. To keep their joyless immaturity going, it becomes good Christian practice to celebrate the birth of Christ, the death of Christ, the resurrection of Christ, and conveniently to forget that all of these events were so that humankind might live with Pentecost joy.

Evidently the first Pentecost was fairly tense. The people standing around thought the men were roaring drunk. Once again Peter was in danger of ridicule or worse, but this time he got up and made a speech of heroic proportions. He began by quoting the prophet Joel: "And in the last days it shall be, God declares, that I will pour out my spirit upon all flesh, and your sons and your daughters shall prophesy, and your young men shall see visions and your old men shall dream dreams" (Acts 2:14-21).

I am particularly fond of this quotation because it so accurately portrays the passion of one overcome with joy. In his joy, Peter not only talked mostly about young people; he talked like a young person. Peter talked of prophecy, visions, and dreams. He talked of fire and smoke; of the sun gone dark and the moon turned to blood. I do not wish to deny the theological meaning of Peter's speech, but I want very much to underscore the language he chose. Peter, the man who had once held back his commitment to Christ under the guise of caution, guilt and naïveté, the man who had lost his pretentious illusions about himself and despaired, now employed the language of a man transformed and transported. For out of crushing loss, he found the Christ he adored created within himself.

Only in their loss were the apostles thrust into something greater than their fond hopes and fantastic wishes. Loss pulled them into a process that made both their own childish strivings and the "reasoned" objectives of Christ's adversaries petty. In loss they were catapulted into the process of growth and transformation, culminating in the experience of Pentecost. On the day of Pentecost the apostles found the joy of the resurrected Christ in themselves.

Who will personify the truth of Christ? We will. We will because through fearful acceptance, hope, disillusionment and loss, we find Christ in ourselves. Unearned moments of Pentecost joy punctuate our day, our life. The process is as ancient as humankind, but the momentary event is as fresh as today. We do not face the world confident in the sum total of our learning. We face the world with fresh memories of Pentecost joy; the experience of having the spirit of the resurrected Christ within ourselves.

Author Information

George Benson received his undergraduate and medical degrees from the University of Cincinnati. He completed his analytic training at the Chicago Psychoanalytic Institute and was one of the early members of the St. Louis Psychoanalytic Institute. His pioneering work in the relationship of psychological and spiritual issues led to speaking engagements around the country and many radio and television appearances. In recent years he has departed from psychoanalytic practice and now works in psychodynamic psychotherapy.

He is the author of *The Silent Self: a journal of spiritual discovery,* a book about his trip to Nepal, published by Forward Movement.